101 FACEBOOK MARKETING TIPS AND STRATEGIES

For Small Businesses

By Lasse Rouhiainen

www.101fb.com

ISBN-13: 978-1530027491

ISBN-10: 1530027497

DOWNLOAD BONUS MATERIAL FOR THIS BOOK

Signup to download the checklist, templates, and other additional resources that will help you to implement the strategies shared in this book:

www.101fb.com/resources

You can share your experience reading this book, or implementing some of the strategies, with the hashtag #101fb on Facebook or Instagram. I would love to read your posts and comments related to the book.

TABLE OF CONTENTS

INTRODUCTION

Would you like to discover the biggest marketing trends in 2016 for growing your business with Facebook, Instagram, and WhatsApp?

Imagine being able to leverage the latest Facebook and Instagram advertising strategies to increase the bottom line for your business.

Have you seen these impressive numbers?

- Facebook: 1.59 billion monthly active users.
- WhatsApp: 1 billion monthly active users.
- Facebook Messenger: 800 million monthly active users.
- Instagram: 400 million monthly active users.

All of these services are owned by Facebook, and together they form a Facebook marketing ecosystem which allows you to access up to 3.79 billion users combined.

The mastery of each of these platforms can give you a competitive edge against your competitors. This guidebook is broken down into 101 tips and strategies you can quickly learn and implement for your business. You won't find boring facts about the history of Facebook or complex theoretical models, but rather specific and proven actions you can take that are highly beneficial for your business.

As a trainer and speaker, I have given Facebook marketing workshops in different corners of the world, from Madrid to Miami and from Dubai to Helsinki, and have met many business owners who are excited to use Facebook,

Instagram and WhatsApp, but are unaware of the correct strategies and techniques to follow.

That is why I wrote this guidebook offering such a large number of tools, techniques and strategies every business owner can quickly apply and benefit from.

After reading this book you will know:

- How to reach more clients and sell more products on Facebook using the best tools and techniques.
- How to spy on how your competitors do their Facebook marketing and avoid making the same mistakes they make.
- What are some of the most beneficial new features on Facebook in 2016.
- How to set up your security and privacy settings correctly for your personal Facebook profile and improve your personal branding on Facebook.
- How to leverage the explosive growth of Facebook video marketing and maximize communication with potential customers.
- Some of the biggest mistakes businesses commit with Facebook advertising and how to avoid them.
- A secret targeting technique which can significantly improve your Facebook advertising campaigns.
- Frequently asked questions and answers that give you a lot of clarity on how to effectively start advertising on Instagram and Facebook.
- Special Facebook Messenger communication strategies that can help you to improve your customer service.

- WhatsApp marketing strategies that helped one company to expand their business internationally and improve their sales.
- And a whole lot more… in total 101 action tips and strategies.

The book is divided into these ten Chapters:

- Chapter 1: Digital Marketing and Facebook Marketing Strategies
- Chapter 2: Customer and Competitor Analysis
- Chapter 3: Facebook Personal Profile Strategies
- Chapter 4: Facebook Business Page Strategies
- Chapter 5: Basic Facebook Advertising Strategies
- Chapter 6: Advanced Facebook Advertising Strategies
- Chapter 7: Facebook Video Marketing Strategies
- Chapter 8: Instagram Marketing Strategies
- Chapter 9: Instagram Advertising Strategies
- Chapter 10: Facebook Messenger and WhatsApp Marketing Strategies

And each of these Chapters is divided into 10 tips. You might enjoy taking time to review the Table of Contents and maybe start from the part which is most crucial or needed for your business, or you can read the whole book from start to finish.

You will also read powerful expert interviews and case studies from the following online marketing experts who share specific strategies you can learn from and apply to your own business:

- Scott Monty on how to use the new Facebook Live Video to communicate with your audience.
- Gideon Shalwick on how to leverage Facebook video advertising.
- Kevin Davis on how to use Facebook video advertising combined with Facebook sweepstakes.
- Charles Kirkland on how to use a special Facebook targeting option which can quickly improve your Facebook ad results and ROI.
- Rocco Alberto Baldassarre on how one specific Instagram advertising strategy generated 343 sales in 30 days.
- Claudia Araujo on how her company expanded internationally by leveraging WhatsApp marketing strategies.

Because I understand that everyone is so busy these days, I also offer three suggested action steps at the end of each Chapter that can help you to quickly get started implementing these strategies for your business.

I hope you enjoy learning about these different Facebook marketing tips and strategies and wish the greatest success in applying them.

Feel free to visit my site at *www.lasserouhiainen.com* and this book site at *www.101fb.com*

CHAPTER 1

Digital Marketing and Facebook Marketing Strategies

In this first Chapter we will look into some Facebook marketing and digital marketing trends that are affecting the way companies do business. The first five are related to digital marketing in general and the last five are trends related to Facebook.

These 10 trends and strategies serve as an introduction and in the following Chapters you will find more detailed tips and strategies related to them.

DIGITAL MARKETING TRENDS

1. Focus on your customer purchase funnel

It used to be that you could just post information in your local newspaper to let people know about your products and services. Today, successful companies need to analyze and create a customer purchase funnel, also called a sales funnel.

Figure 1.1 illustrates this point. It shows a sample sales funnel showcasing three different levels customers go through before buying your product.

- **Leads - People who see your content or information:** These people maybe have seen your Facebook ad, but are not taking action since it's the first time they've been exposed to your company and need more information in order to move the next phase.

- **Prospects - People who become interested but are not ready to buy yet:** These people are comparing options and typically need more interaction to generate trust with your company.

- **Customers - People who bought your product:** Your task is to identify what special characteristics they have, in order to target these kinds of people with your Facebook promotions, and to communicate with them to try to get them to endorse your product to their friends.

Figure 1.1: Sample sales funnel.

Companies with products that have high transaction values tend to have more levels in their marketing funnels, while companies with low priced products have simple sales funnels, as presented inFigure 1.1.

A central component of the successful sales funnel is email marketing, since it allows you to capture your leads' information and keep in touch with them. You should segment customer information in your email marketing tool or CRM (customer relationship management tool) so that you know how many people your company has in each level of the sales funnel.

HOW YOU CAN HELP CUSTOMERS MOVE TO THE NEXT PHASE IN THE MARKETING FUNNEL

Here is a list of items which help customers to move faster toward the next phase in the funnel and toward the purchase decision:

- Give valuable content for free: This content can be in different forms and needs to be interesting and relevant to the initial problem that the customer has.
- Offer more opportunities for engagement: Customers need more opportunities to communicate with your company on different platforms.
- Generate trust and credibility: Share customer experiences and case studies. Survey your buyers and ask why they bought your products, and use that information to improve your funnel.
- Track results in each level of the funnel: Analyze the results in each level of the funnel and use that data to improve and modify your funnel.

2. Accept the fact that consumers' attention spans are getting shorter

The strong growth of the usage of portable mobile devices and digitalized lifestyles in general has significantly changed the way people consume content on the Internet. According to several studies, consumers' attention spans are getting shorter all the time and companies need to adapt their marketing strategies for this new trend.

- **Make content that is easy to consume:** Typically this means creating shorter content so that consumers can consume it before getting distracted and moving to the next thing. With content I refer to videos, photos, GIFs and articles, just to name few. A long form content still has its place for consumers who already know you and your company, but for most new potential clients you need to create short and interesting content.

- **Make the beginning of your content count:** The first paragraphs of your article or the first 4 seconds of a video are the most important, as you need to invite consumers to consume the rest of your content. Using questions in the beginning of your content normally helps to get consumers' attention.

One strategy to tackle the shorter attention span is to generate content that is highly personalized and relevant. It is also very important to learn how to analyze the results and modify your content accordingly.

In general, the greatest challenge right now is how to capture and keep people's attention when they view your content. Smart companies are already adapting their content accordingly and you should do the same.

3. Have more customer contact points

Traditionally it used to be sufficient for companies to only have a website, but today consumers demand more engagement and communication via different points of contact and pieces of content before they perceive your company as trustworthy.

These customer contact points are also called touch points, and here is an example of how Facebook allows businesses to connect with clients using multiple touch points:

- Imagine that you share information and content with the client on your Facebook Business Page.
- After that, the client goes to Instagram and sees your new video which is related to the content he or she already saw on your Facebook Business Page.
- After that, the client will send a WhatsApp message to you or contact you via the Facebook Messenger app to ask for more details about your product.

Interestingly, all the platforms mentioned in this example (Facebook Page, Instagram, WhatsApp and Facebook Messenger) pertain to the Facebook ecosystem. One of Facebook's goals is to create more tools for small businesses so that companies can generate more business within the Facebook ecosystem.

4. Recognize the increasing importance of paid advertising

In today's world, customers are turning away from impulse-buying and want to learn more about a company before buying its products. Customers are often distracted, but recognize that they have a choice when it comes to the businesses they choose to support, so they tend to require more touch points (or points of contact) with the companies they buy from. Paid advertising is the best way to meet these needs.

Online paid advertising, and most specifically, advertising through Facebook, can offer a great way to generate new leads, targeting potential customers who have not yet interacted with your brand, and to stay in contact with your current customers, letting them know about additional products or services that may be helpful to them.

It's not always about making a sale with paid advertising. Sometimes, just ensuring that the customer is mindful of what your company is doing can indirectly increase sales. With great tools like paid advertising through Facebook, you can increase the impact of your business, expanding your reach through simple content. Few companies are able to grow quickly without implementing paid advertising strategies.

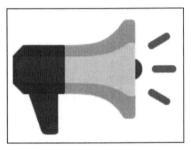

Figure 1.2: Facebook advertising.

There are costs associated with advertising online, but the good news is that you can start small and calculate your returns fairly easily. Facebook is constantly improving their tools, and it is simple to start using them.

All of the companies that are currently dominating their industries are using paid advertising, and many of them rely on Facebook advertising. In the modern market, I would highly recommend that all businesses, new or old, use this method of advertising to grow their brand.

5. Recognize the huge impact virtual reality will have for businesses

Remember a few years back when you needed to visit the Facebook website on your desktop computer to go to your Facebook account? Nowadays, you can do the same more quickly by simply opening the Facebook application on your mobile device.

However, in the future it is quite possible that in order to login to Facebook, you would put on a virtual headset, showing you content from your Facebook friends in a much more immersive way, making you feel as if you are actually right there with your friends. It will still take some time before we are there, but it is quite likely to happen.

Facebook's founder and CEO Mark Zuckerberg has long been fascinated with the future possibilities of virtual reality, and in 2014 Facebook purchased a virtual reality company called Oculus VR. Their new virtual reality device – Oculus Rift – retails for the price of $599 USD and will be used for a number of marketing activities in the future.

Currently, virtual reality is mainly known in the gaming industry, but in the future it will provide huge opportunities for the entertainment, travel, real estate, automotive, education, and many other industries. Today, the tools and software for creating and consuming content for virtual reality devices are still a bit expensive, but as the prices come down, more and more companies will start to use them.

Figure 1.3: Virtual reality.

At this moment, most of the marketing is being done with still images or 2-dimensional videos (most of the videos you see online are two dimensional), but Facebook is preparing a more immersive opportunity that allows consumers to feel that they are actually somewhere else when wearing a virtual reality device. Virtual reality will greatly help companies to communicate the benefits of their products and services. The implications of this for marketing are huge and the companies that adapt first will reap enormous benefits.

In addition to Facebook, other big technology companies like Apple, Google and Amazon are also working on virtual reality, which will make the adaptation of this next phase of technology faster.

FACEBOOK MARKETING TRENDS

6. Learn to leverage the opportunities in the Facebook ecosystem

At the moment, Facebook is the biggest social network, serving over 1.5 billion active users each month, and also owns several other social media tools, including Instagram (with 400 million active users), WhatsApp (1 billion active users), and Facebook Messenger (800 million active users). Each of these tools provides a unique and powerful way to interact and engage with your potential customers.

Each of these tools will be covered in detail later in this book, but here is a quick overview of the Facebook ecosystem for businesses:

- **Facebook:** Every business that wants to leverage marketing opportunities available through social media should have a Facebook Business Page. The proper use of a Facebook personal profile helps tremendously in personal branding of business professionals. In addition, Facebook advertising offers unlimited possibilities to reach more customers.

- **Instagram**: Instagram is growing quickly and has become a potent tool to serve industries that offer visual products. Their advertising tools are highly effective for all types of businesses.

- **WhatsApp:** This is an amazing tool to provide one-to-one communication with customers, especially when they want to gain more information before making a purchase. Businesses have reported that it has made them more successful in building trust and brand loyalty with their customers. It is important, however, not to use WhatsApp for unsolicited messages or spam.

- **Facebook Messenger:** Facebook is constantly updating this tool to ensure that it optimizes communications between businesses and their customers. You can use it to send text, video, or audio messages, and this tool will continue to be developed toward customer support in the future.

In order to grow your business, the best strategy is to use all four of these tools together. While there is a slight learning curve to each tool, they are worth the time and energy invested into them. Because some of these tools are fairly new, companies that explore and invest in these tools early on can gain a competitive edge over others in their industries.

7. Take advantage of the explosive growth of video marketing on Facebook

Video can be a very effective tool for gaining trust and credibility with your customers. In many cases, consumers are more comfortable making a purchase decision if they've been able to view a video about the product or service beforehand. In the past, there weren't as many opportunities for consumers to see videos, due to low Internet connection speeds, but now, the video marketing possibilities have increased drastically, especially for mobile viewers.

Video marketing through Facebook offers several unique benefits:

- **Expand the reach of your business through video content:** Facebook promotes video content over more static content, like photos or status update, allowing video content to reach more users.

- **Create transparency through live video streaming:** One of the new tools from Facebook is the Facebook Mentions app, which allows businesses to post live videos. This is a great way to allow your customers to see you respond to questions, show a demo of a product, or give a behind-the-scenes look at your office, creating a sense of transparency.

- **Impress potential customers with rich, 360-degree video:** Give your customers a whole new way to see your company through their News Feed. With this tool, the user is in control of the video and can move around the room by tilting their phone or clicking around in it on their desktop. This is a great way for hotels and other location-based businesses to provide a powerful visual.

- **Increase sales conversions through video advertising:** Video advertising can be fairly inexpensive and offers numerous possibilities, including simple product demonstrations and testimonial videos. With a great reach and not a lot of competition, you can increase your sales dramatically when you use Facebook video advertising.

In the future, we can expect even more great tools for video marketing from Facebook. They have already expanded into creative video tools with virtual reality devices like Oculus Rift, and have goals to become the top video marketing site on the Internet, surpassing YouTube.

Video is one of the most powerful tools available to advertisers right now, as we'll explore more in a later Chapter of this book.

8. No website needed: take advantage of the new business tools from Facebook

Recently, Facebook has introduced several tools to help businesses bypass the need for a traditional website and take advantage of sales driven directly through the social network. This is a new approach to advertising, and companies that are on the forefront of this trend can drive sales in unique ways.

Here are the four primary tools for businesses provided by Facebook:

- **Facebook Business Page:** This tool has been around on Facebook for a while, but new features are constantly available. A Facebook Business Page replaces a traditional landing page as the primary method for Facebook users to interact with a business.
- **Facebook Canvas:** This is a brand-new tool being developed by Facebook that will be launched soon, as of the time of this writing. It will provide professional tools to help companies to showcase their products. To learn more, visit *https://canvas.facebook.com*.
- **Facebook Local Advertising:** These ads include a direct call-to-action, so that customers can see an advertisement and respond directly, requesting a quote, making a reservation, or performing a number of actions that used to require a separate website.
- **Facebook Local Services:** In this tool, Facebook provides a listing of local businesses for which

customers can leave reviews. It is similar to the services offered by Yelp and Google Local, but is driven by Facebook. Learn more about this tool at *https://www.facebook.com/services*.

Figure 1.4: Screenshot of Facebook Canvas at https://canvas.facebook.com.

Companies can also communicate and engage with their customers through Facebook Messenger or WhatsApp, allowing all of the layers of advertising to come into one central place, which will ultimately help to increase the rate of sales conversions from your advertising efforts.

9. No phone number needed – leverage communication tools with Facebook Messenger and WhatsApp

The way that consumers communicate is changing rapidly, as new tools are available that allow for quick, meaningful interactions. Instant messaging tools for mobile devices have grown exponentially, and along with them, tools like Facebook Messenger (with over 800 million users) and the

Facebook-owned WhatsApp (with over 1 billion users) are growing too.

These tools are helpful because they don't require you to have phone numbers for your clients. You can contact customers directly through the Facebook Messenger service, communicating in more ways than ever before: Sending photos, videos, GIFs, or even directions to your business.

For many customers, this is quickly becoming their preferred method of communication, since they no longer have to deal with the awkwardness of cold calls. It also allows customers to interact on the go, using their mobile device apps or a desktop device by visiting *www.messenger.com*. These tools also allow you to communicate with your clients in richer and more meaningful ways.

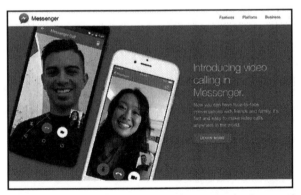

Figure 1.5: Screenshot of Facebook Messenger that can be found at www.messenger.com.

Additionally, the new Businesses on Messenger service is now available through Facebook to certain companies in the United States. This service allows businesses to create custom message layouts and to provide better customer support tools. More information about this helpful tool will be available at the end of this book.

10. Analyze your results on the Facebook ecosystem

In the past, a business could only calculate their impact on Facebook through the number of "likes" their pages received. While marketing activities are now more complex, businesses have the capability to analyze a number of interactions and see the direct results of their advertising efforts on Facebook.

It is important to have clarity on what you are looking for from each tool so that you can calculate your return on investment. For example, if a customer responded to a Facebook ad and purchased a $20 product and you spent $5 to advertise, your return on investment would be $15. Over time, if you can, also track the total lifetime value of a client for even more accurate returns.

Start analyzing your results from the minute you start to use Facebook for your business. There are several ways to do this:

- On your business page, see what kinds of content have the most engagement and use this information to create future content.
- With Facebook advertising campaigns, track the ads that are running well and adapt or delete the ads that are not as effective.
- For video marketing, look at the video retention rate to see how many users are watching the video to completion.

- With WhatsApp and Facebook Messenger, keep an eye on the number of contacts your business has received, how many purchases resulted from your interactions, and what quality of lead (or potential buyer) came from your contact.

Each of these tools will be covered in detail later on.

THREE SUGGESTED ACTION STEPS FROM CHAPTER 1:

After each Chapter I share three recommended action steps. Try to do these exercises before moving to the next Chapter of the book. You can also use the templates offered in the resource package of this book.

- Think about which phases of the sales funnel your business has. Try to draw an example of it. Analyze what type of content or communication you should use in each of those phases.

- Consider how you could create content that catches consumers' attention fast, as their attention span is becoming shorter.

- Make a list of ideas about how you could have more touch points with your clients and communicate better with them.

CHAPTER 2

Customer and Competitor Analysis

Modern Facebook marketing always begins by analyzing your ideal client, and determining which online tools would be most effective for better identifying the ideal customer, as well as the competition. This Chapter provides five strategies for customer analysis, and another five strategies for gathering competitive intelligence.

STRATEGIES RELATED TO CUSTOMER ANALYSIS

11. Create your customer avatar

Before implementing Facebook marketing strategies, you need to first get a clear picture of who your ideal client will be. Obviously, your products and services are available for everyone to buy; but, in today's over-competitive business environment, you need to be extremely clear as to whom you want to reach and who would be your ideal client.

When creating your customer avatar, these are some of the areas you need to identify:

Basic information:

- **Age & gender:** What is the gender and age range of your most profitable buyers?
- **Geographic location:** Where are your best clients located? For example, while one e-commerce store might determine that their best clients live in a certain region of the country, a local clothing store might

find that their customer basis lives in one particular area of the city.

- **Interests categories:** What are your targeted clients' hobbies and interests? Which magazines do they buy? Which TV programs do they watch?
- **Websites they visit:** What are the biggest web portals, news sites, or blogs that your clients visit?

More specific information:

- **Motivation to buy:** What really incentivizes your clients to make purchasing decisions? For example, someone who wants to buy a course on how to stop smoking is probably also interested in the broader category of improving his or her health, not just quitting smoking.
- **Main problem:** What is your client's main problem or challenge he or she wants to resolve?
- **Emotional need related to the problem:** What is the emotional need related to the main problem your ideal client wants to resolve? For example, single women who want to lose weight might have an emotional need of finding a life partner.
- **Keywords:** When using Google or other search engines, what keywords do your ideal clients most use?

For most businesses, creating a client avatar with such "basic information" is sufficient. The "specific information" section normally takes more time, and is possible to do without. Regardless, the most common mistake business owners commit – notwithstanding the level of detail – is creating just one avatar. I recommend trying to create at least three different customer avatars.

12. Conduct basic research on Facebook Pages

Only a few business owners actually spend the time analyzing how other companies leverage Facebook marketing before implementing their own strategies. However, this type of basic research enables you to clarify what type of content and communication works best in your sector, and is worth the time taken.

The following is a very basic Facebook marketing research strategy you may implement. You can create a simple Excel spreadsheet to gather and organize all of this information.

Visit Facebook Pages in your sector and analyze the following characteristics of their content:

- Written text:
- What words are most used to start a Facebook post?
- What kinds of calls to action do they use?
- Do they post short sentences or long paragraphs?
- Do they use specific words or verbiage related to your sector?
- Photos: Do they upload photos that are beautiful and well-edited?
- Content: How often do they post?
- Videos: What kinds of videos do they use?
- Engagement: Which of their content has the most comments, likes, and shares?
- Other observations?

You may also analyze what kinds of cover photos they use, and what types of basic information they provide on their Facebook Pages.

Are you having difficulty finding Facebook Pages for companies in your sector? Later in this Chapter we will cover tools like SocialBakers and Likealyzer which help locate such companies for analysis. As discussed later, I recommend running such research for three different groups: (1) companies in your sector; (2) your biggest competitors; and (3) the most popular Facebook Pages in your country. Basic research like this might sound boring, but it is a must for effective Facebook marketing (and can be outsourced if you prefer).

13. Constantly analyze Facebook Page Insights

Facebook Page insights can be found for every Facebook Page, and business owners should examine the data provided by this tool every week. Page insights allows you to know what type of content your audience liked best, and what part of your audience is most engaged.

With this tool you will find information on three key indicators related to your Facebook Page: likes, reach, and engagement. Every Facebook Page owner should continuously find new methods of increasing engagement and, therefore, these metrics are probably the most significant when analyzing what kind of content generated the most. There are also useful metrics for videos posted on your Facebook Page which we will cover later in this book.

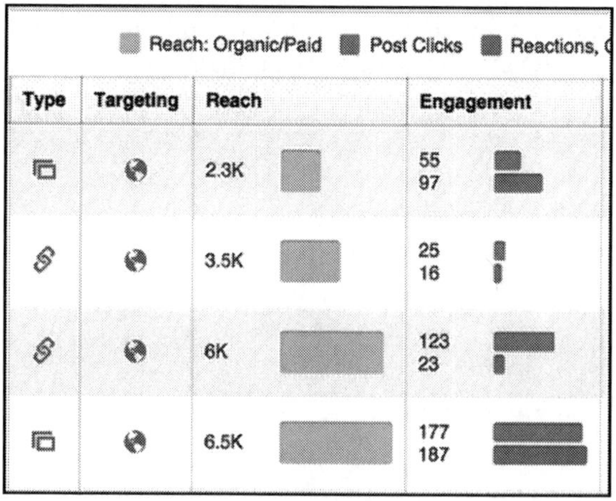

Type	Targeting	Reach		Engagement	
			Reach: Organic/Paid	Post Clicks	Reactions,

Type	Targeting	Reach		Engagement	
▣	🌐	2.3K		55 97	
✦	🌐	3.5K		25 16	
✦	🌐	6K		123 23	
▣	🌐	6.5K		177 187	

Figure 2.1: Facebook Page insights shows the type of content that generates most engagement among your audience.

The People section of Facebook Page insights gives information regarding the age, gender and geographic location of your Facebook fans. This data is vital for creating targeted campaigns with your Facebook advertising.

14. Obtain precious customer data from Audience Insights

In 2014, Facebook launched a free tool which helps determine who your ideal clients are, their interests, and their buying habits. This is an indispensable tool for both Facebook advertisers and Page owners, and provides a lot of behavioral and demographic data.

You should use this data not only to craft more specific customer avatars, but also to gain valuable insights into your competitors.

Facebook Audience Insights can be found at _www.facebook.com/ads/audience_insights_. To start, you need to select one of the following audience types you want to analyze:

- All Facebook users.
- People connected to your Facebook Page.
- A Custom Audience (this term will be explained in the Facebook Advertising Chapter of this book).

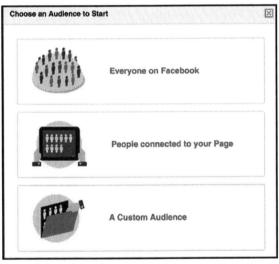

Figure 2.2: Three audience options you can select when using Facebook Audience Insights.

You can only analyze one audience at a time. Obtaining information about the people who are connected to your Page is vital, but for your analysis with this tool it's best to start with everyone on Facebook.

Suppose you have an online business selling yoga training and you are eager to gain data regarding people who are interested in yoga. First, select everyone on Facebook as the audience type, and then enter "yoga" below the field which says "interests" (see the image below).

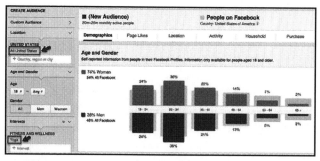

Figure 2.3: Demographic data showcased by Facebook Audience Insights on people who are interested on yoga.

According to the demographic data for Facebook users throughout the USA, 74% of people who are interested in yoga are women and 26% are men. Therefore, the focus of your Facebook content and advertising should be directed primarily toward women.

The navigation bar for this tool (at the top) provides even more revealing information, such as:

- Pages liked and followed (Page Likes).
- Geographical location (Location).
- Activity, i.e., comments, likes, etc. (Activity).
- Household data (Household).
- Purchase behavior (Purchase).

Data regarding household and purchase behavior is provided by third-party companies (not Facebook itself), and currently only works for searches within the USA.

Take at least 30 minutes to get familiar with this tool; it is immensely powerful for gaining data and insights about your sector which your competitors probably don't yet know.

15. Discover valuable insights by surveying your clients

Surprisingly few small businesses conduct surveys, although they are probably the most valuable strategy for obtaining information about your ideal clients.

Surveys can be run for people who are signed up for your newsletter or are fans of your Facebook Page. I would create a separate survey for customers who have purchased a product or service from you.

Here are some questions you should ask your Facebook fans:

- What kind of Facebook content would they most like your company to provide?
- Do they have any specific questions related to your product or service?
- What other Facebook Pages or websites do they follow and why?

Here are some questions you should ask your buyers:

- What did they like most about your product or service?
- What did they dislike about your product or service?
- What other products would they like to buy?

Each company should run these kinds of surveys at least once per fiscal quarter. Two tools you can consider for conducting such a service include: SurveyMonkey® *www.surveymonkey.com* (paid) and Google Forms *www.google.com/forms* (free).

STRATEGIES RELATED TO COMPETITOR AND INDUSTRY ANALYSIS

16. Get the latest Facebook data on your industry from SocialBakers

SocialBakers is a social media analytics and publishing company that provides data and analytics on how Facebook is used in different industries and regions. Most of the reports are free - you are just prompted to sign up for a free account.

Industry Reports

SocialBakers industry reports reveal some key information, such as: Facebook marketing benchmarks, top Facebook posts, and the fastest growing Facebook brands in each industry. Every business owner should spend at least one hour each month analyzing the data and trends provided in these reports. Doing so will enable you to discover the brands with the most effective Facebook marketing. These reports are typically updated on a monthly basis and cover activity for all global brands in each particular industry. You can find the SocialBakers industry reports at:
www.socialbakers.com/resources/reports/industry.

Figure 2.4: Screenshot of SocialBakers industry report of food & beverages industry.

Country Statistics

In addition to industry reports, SocialBakers also provides information related to brand marketing, and which ones are producing the most effective Facebook engagement and reach. I find this information remarkable as it allows you to find successful models which can be tracked to help adapt and improve your own content.

SocialBakers country statistics can be found at:
www.socialbakers.com/statistics/facebook/pages/total/brands.

17. Use Likealyzer to discover companies that dominate Facebook marketing

Likealyzer is one of the most effective free tools for analyzing the competition. Found at *www.likealyzer.com*, this program enables you to see how your efforts rank against others' within your industry. Simply enter your Facebook Page URL within the search field and click "enter." This tool will provide you with a list of recommendations on how to improve your Page, along with other useful data, through analysis and ranking of every Facebook Page. This tool also provides a rare listing of some of the best performing Facebook Pages, sorted by both country and industry.

Let's say you have a clothing company in Canada and want to obtain insights as to how other companies in your industry use Facebook. Go to *www.likealyzer.com/statistics*, and select "clothing" as the category and "Canada" as the subject country. Likealyze will provide a list of the most effective Facebook Pages within that industry and region - which you can then visit and analyze.

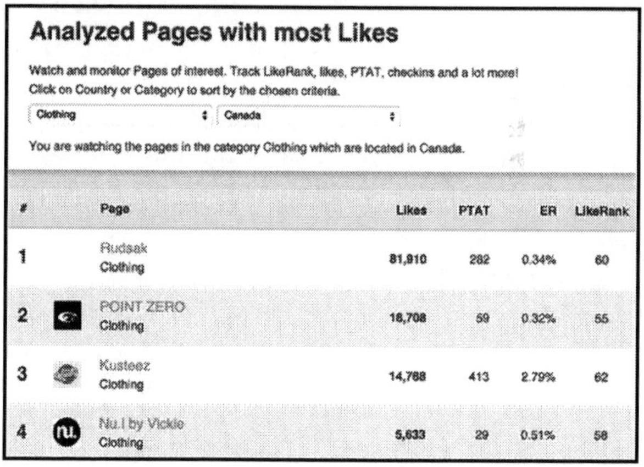

Analyzed Pages with most Likes

Watch and monitor Pages of interest. Track LikeRank, likes, PTAT, checkins and a lot more!
Click on Country or Category to sort by the chosen criteria.

Clothing	Canada

You are watching the pages in the category Clothing which are located in Canada.

#	Page	Likes	PTAT	ER	LikeRank
1	Rudsak Clothing	81,910	282	0.34%	60
2	POINT ZERO Clothing	18,708	59	0.32%	55
3	Kusteez Clothing	14,768	413	2.79%	62
4	Nu.I by Vickie Clothing	5,633	29	0.51%	58

Figure 2.5: Screenshot of Likealyzer statistics for clothing companies in Canada
www.likealyzer.com/statistics/facebook/likes/category/Clothing/country/Canada.

I recommend spending at least 30 minutes analyzing the best companies in your sector, visiting their Facebook Pages and documenting the following:

- What kind of text do they use?
- What kind of photos do they post?
- What kind of videos do they create and share?
- What other strategies do they use that you yourself find interesting?

Do the same research across a few other sectors or countries as well to gain additional creative ideas for your own Facebook content.

18. Find content, news stories, and influence by using Buzzsumo

Interested in quickly finding the latest news stories, compelling content, and people with influence in your sector? Buzzsumo, which can be found at *www.buzzsumo.com*, is an excellent research tool that allows you to find top trending viral content.

FIND TOPICS FOR ARTICLES PEOPLE WANT TO READ AND SHARE WITH THEIR FRIENDS

You can type any keyword on Buzzsumo and get a list of the top shared or commented on articles, blogs, or media content. You can also filter the results by date range, location, or language, as well as by the social media platform used. The screenshot image below shows the top results for a search of the term "Italian Food."

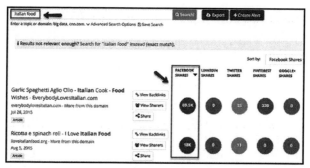

Figure 2.6: Results for the search term Italian food on Buzzsumo.com.

Information like this is extremely valuable for finding content ideas and news stories within your sector. You can share these stories on your Facebook Page, or create your own content based on them.

FIND OUT THE MOST POPULAR CONTENT ON YOUR COMPETITORS' WEBSITES.

Buzzsumo also allows you to search specific URL links (i.e., your competitors' websites) to find what content is most shared by them on social media. Perform this research for at least five of your competitors' websites and you will quickly learn what content your target audience most wants to see.

Buzzsumo's free version is limited to a few searches per day. The paid pro version allows for unlimited searches and offers extra features.

19. Obtain valuable client insights with Google Trends

Google Trends is a leading research tool for many online marketers, tracking all Google web keyword searches by regional interest. In other words, analytics are provided for which areas most search for a specific term or phrase. For example, using "mountain bike" as the relevant search term, Google Trends provides the below breakdown of location interest:

Figure 2.7: Google Trends results for the keyword "Mountain Bike".

In the above search, Google Trends shows that the term "mountain bike" was predominantly searched by people in the western United States, ranking Colorado, Utah, Montana, and Wyoming as the top four. This type of information is crucial for Facebook marketing, allowing Page owners to create better-targeted Facebook advertising campaigns, and to obtain overall better information about their ideal clients.

Google Trends is a free tool and can be found at *www.google.com/trends*

20. Discover keywords your clients search online

Keyword research is an activity related to search engine optimization (SEO) for websites, but reveals interesting data for Facebook Page owners as well. This type of analysis tracks phrases that people most search on Google and other search engines. WordTracker, one of the most respected keyword tools, provides a list of terms your ideal client is searching.

Suppose you are a real estate agent in London. Simply go to *www.wordtracker.com* and type "London property." The result is a list of keywords most frequently searched online with that topic. Though predominantly used for search engine optimization, the same can be useful in optimizing Facebook Page content. Find terms most searched, incorporate them into your own content, and attract more visitors through search results.

Keyword	Volume
london commercial property	136
property management london	48
property investors london	38
property maintenance london	38
commercial property london	32
property developers london	26
off plan property london	23
london property surveyors	23
london property lease	20
property market london 2015	6

Figure 2.8: Keyword list on "London property" provided by WordTracker.com

THREE SUGGESTED ACTION STEPS FROM CHAPTER 2:

Here are three suggested action steps related to the content of this Chapter. Try to complete these before moving to the next Chapter.

- Create your basic customer avatar following the recommendations in strategy 11. Try to add some more specific information like *motivation to buy or emotional need related to the problem.*

- Conduct some basic research on Facebook by visiting the Business Pages of your competitors and analyzing the points mentioned in strategy 12.

- Set aside enough time to visit the statistics on SocialBakers.com and also analyze the companies in your sector using Likealyzer (strategy 13).

CHAPTER 3

Facebook Personal Profile Strategies

The following Chapter provides key strategies to help optimize professional branding and networking through the use of a personal Facebook profile. Although not an exhaustive list, the tips and tactics discussed here are some of the most valuable on which to focus your efforts at this stage (including, but not limited to, various privacy and security settings). For a review of business Facebook profiles, refer to Chapter four of this book.

21. Get clear on how your personal profile can support your business objectives

Most people use their Facebook profile only to connect with family and friends, not realizing that Facebook offers numerous business applications as well. So, before applying the specific strategies shared in this Chapter it's worth it to first get clarity on how the use of a Facebook profile can support your business objectives. For most business professionals, the greatest benefit is networking - with both valuable new business contacts as well as current connections - through sharing interesting pictures, videos, and articles that can further enhance their brand.

To summarize, some typical benefits of correctly using a personal Facebook profile for professional aims include:

- Improved professional network.
- Improved reputation among other professionals in your sector.
- Opportunity to share valuable information related to your company and products.

Start setting aside some time to think over your business objectives, and the specific aspects you'd like your Facebook profile activity to support.

22. Keep your profile up-to-date

Tools like Facebook are only as good as the information you provide. Try to keep your Facebook profile information current, with all of the relevant information you want people to find out about you. If you use your Facebook profile for both personal reasons and business networking, it is best to avoid sharing too much personal data, such as who your family members are or where you live.

Many employers have gotten into the habit of investigating candidates' Facebook profiles. Whether you're in the market for new work or just expanding your network, you should be sharing correct and updated professional information (including past experience and skills). Your personal page can also share contact details and links to your professional website and other social networks, along with a short introduction about who you are as a business professional.

Facebook pages are tracked by username, so you may wish to revise the default hyperlink assigned to your name. You can do so by visiting *www.facebook.com/username* and selecting a preferred alternative.

23. Optimize your privacy settings

As a basic matter, every Facebook user should review and update his or her privacy settings, found at:

www.facebook.com/settings. These should be customized to your personal preferences, including what other Facebook users have access to seeing. Currently, Facebook allows configuration of three different sections:

- Who can see my stuff?
- Who can contact me?
- Who can look me up?

A screenshot image of this page is provided below.

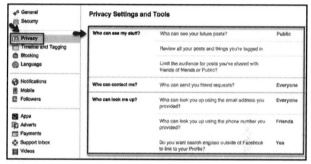

Figure 3.1: A screenshot image of Facebook's privacy settings and tools.

If as a business professional you want to maximize promotion of a personal brand, the broadest category is to allow everyone to see every post (found in the "who can see my stuff" section) and to allow search engines to generate links to the profile (in the "who can look me up" section). As previously stated, if you do provide such broad access, for safety reasons you should be sure to review and restrict the personal information provided on your page (i.e., home address). To the contrary, privacy settings can also be optimized more openly for those who connect primarily with personal and family members.

It's important to note that Facebook frequently updates and revises the site's privacy terms and settings. It would therefore be advisable that you visit these sections every month to confirm that all settings are configured according to your preferences.

24. Optimize your Facebook security settings

Hacking – the threat of someone accessing your private Facebook account. Today, the threat is all too real and provides many personal security concerns. Luckily, Facebook has created an additional security setting to further protect the user's private access to his or her account – in the form of personalized security codes.

When a user has a security code on file, Facebook will verify the location from where your account is accessed. If a new and unknown location is used, a notification to that effect is generated and is sent to the email account on file corresponding to that security code. If it is in fact you, you simply provide the code and authorize the location. If it is not you, then the unknown user cannot go any further.

A screenshot image of this page is provided below.

Figure 3.2: Screenshot image of Facebook's security settings.

The primary security features have been outlined above. Ultimately, it is your choice how little or how much public access you want to create. However, I would recommend everyone to use at least the first three security settings: *login alerts, login approvals and code generator.*

Finally, I note the importance of new passwords. Security features such as the above protect one aspect of your privacy, but periodically renewing your password always provides another. Keep a record of your change (but do not save it in your email inbox), and always log-out of Facebook when using a public computer.

25. Design an effective profile cover image

One of the first things people see when visiting a Facebook profile is the cover image. Most business professionals focus on creating a professional cover image for the business page, but neglect doing the same for a personal profile.

Here are some tips to follow when designing the cover image for your profile.

- Use the correct image size: 851 x 315 pixels.
- A collage of several images may be used, but try to create a focus on yourself for visual connection by the user.
- Keep it clean and to the point, limiting the amount of text.
- You may wish to use a tool, such as Canva, to quickly create a professional profile image (this example of an online tool also offers free templates you can use, which can be found at: *www.canva.com/create/facebook-covers*).

Try to make a cover image which is related to your work but still personal at the same time. For example, if you are a public speaker, you can create an image including several pictures of your speaking engagements and with a short call to action indicating how people can contact you. You can also change the cover image throughout the year, and may wish to take advantage of a certain holiday or seasonal theme.

26. Use the Facebook mobile applications

Facebook offers several mobile applications (both on iPhone and Android), which allow you to use Facebook more effectively on a mobile device. Following are the three such most important tools:

- **Facebook mobile application:** This enables you to do all of the basic Facebook functions, i.e., add friends, and share pictures, videos, and updates.

- **Facebook messenger application:** The Messenger app lets you quickly send and receive messages from Facebook friends. Additionally, this app allows you to make free video calls or leave voice messages for people who have also installed the application. This method of messaging can vastly improve the quality of your communication, with audio and video formats more quickly building trust and credibility over basic text. Your previous correspondences can also be saved, allowing you to revisit past interactions with your clients and to confirm details mentioned in earlier messages.

- **Facebook group application:** If you are member of Facebook Groups, this application enables you to interact with them all and to remain active while on the go. The functionality of this program is more effective than the default Facebook app.

Remember always to update your apps to the latest versions. The above Facebook mobile applications and others can be found at: *www.facebook.com/mobile*.

27. Get followers and follow interesting people on Facebook

Facebook has created a limit on the number of friends per user (5,000), after which no more new requests may be accepted. However, a few years back, Facebook introduced a new "Follow" feature, which allows you to follow people's posts without actually being their "friend." This addition has proven highly useful for celebrities and publicFigures, and works just as well for the general public – including those who want to grow a large following on Facebook for their personal profile.

Robert Scoble, a well-known tech blogger and early adopter of this feature, has notably collected more than 670,000 followers of his personal Facebook profile (*www.facebook.com/RobertScoble*). He regularly shares interesting news and updates related to technology, which people have been able to follow and stay updated on without actually "friending" this man. This is a great example of how powerful the above-mentioned feature can truly be for your own needs and goals.

To follow someone, search their name and visit their profile, then click on "follow." You should immediately start to see their posts on your News Feed. You can visit a list of suggestions to follow at: *www.facebook.com/follow/suggestions*.

To get people to follow you, visit *www.facebook.com/settingsand* and click "followers" in the left column. Here, you can configure all of the settings related to followers as well as add a button link on your website which allows people to follow you.

Settings related to followers can be found at: www.facebook.com/settings. You can also learn more about the Facebook Follow feature here at *www.facebook.com/about/follow*.

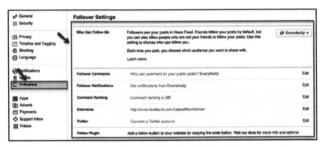

Figure 3.3: Screenshot of Facebook's Follower settings.

28. Share your articles using Facebook Notes

Have you written an interesting article that you'd like to share with Facebook friends and followers? In addition to photos, videos, and short text messages on your Facebook profile, the updated Facebook Notes feature allows you also to add articles. Notes can be used for both personal profiles and business Facebook pages.

To see how the Facebook Notes feature works, visit *www.facebook.com/notes* and observe Notes already created by your Facebook friends or people you follow. At the top of the same page you can create your own Note, see Notes you have previously written, or review and edit your drafts.

*Figure 3.4: You can create a Note by visiting
www.facebook.com/notes and clicking on Write a note.*

Before publishing a Note, plan and define its objective. Is there any call to action you want to give to people? Perhaps you have a specific agenda or goal with that particular post? Avoid being overly promotional of your product. Instead, try to provide useful information to your readers, with great visuals, and in a manner that's easy to read. At the end of the article you can then send people to your blog post or website which offers the promotional information.

Most of your readers are busy people, likely viewing your Notes from a mobile device. Therefore, try to enhance their reading experience by offering short paragraphs or bullet points. You may even wish to start and end your Note with an engaging question to encourage engaged reading.

The following example is a Note shared by technology investor Loic Le Meur:

Figure 3.5: Example of a Note

As you can see from the example, the cover image is quite prominently displayed (1200 pixels wide by 445 pixels high). Select yours wisely.

29. Take advantage of Facebook Live Video

Facebook video is a relatively new content format, and is already generating some of the greatest engagement on Facebook. Coming soon in 2016, Facebook will also be offering a live video feature (called Facebook Mentions) for most profiles and business pages. Mobile live video streaming applications, like Periscope and Meetkat, have been growing quickly and so Facebook will be offering the same opportunity to keep pace.

Strategic communications consultant Scott Monty conducts a live videoconference every Sunday sharing news of the communications and marketing industry. Scott's followers can view the video and interact live, and also see the recording later on Scott's Facebook profile. This is a proper example of taking advantage of the new

Facebook feature and sharing valuable content on a personal Facebook profile.

Figure 3.6: Screenshot of live video streaming by Scott Monty.

Here are a few tips from Scott Monty, which might help you to start your live streaming on Facebook.

EXPERT OPINION – Scott Monty

"Facebook Mentions makes live video possible for Pages, and while live video is powerful, absent a strategy it can be a dangerous thing. It's quite simple for anyone (or any brand) to pop open the app and start streaming. But before doing so, brands should have an idea of what they hope to achieve: awareness, community building, customer service, or something else."

EXPERT OPINION – Scott Monty (*continued*)

"Examples of how these strategies might be brought to life include: giving exclusive information to followers, such as a behind-the-scenes tour; making executives available for an interview and Q&A-style interaction; live customer service hours; a product reveal.

The live stream need not be a perfect high-production video, but it does need to be better than amateur hour. A shaky camera will lessen your credibility and poor audio will make it difficult for people to follow along. Just be aware of the minimum requirements for live video and be sure you're covered. With this and a solid strategy, you should be off to a great start to building stronger relationships with your customers."

Scott Monty,
Strategic Communications Consultant
www.scottmonty.com

30. Understand the importance of the new Facebook Reaction Emojis

Facebook has long been using the "Like" button that helps users to quickly indicate which content they like. At the time of writing this book they are introducing new emojis, also called Facebook Reactions. These are pictorial representations of facial expressions, giving Facebook users the ability to quickly show their emotions, for example anger or sympathy, related to any content they see. Facebook is implementing these emojis now, as most Facebook users access the social network from their mobile phones and emojis serve as a quick way to express their emotions without the need to write something.

You will find a way to show your reaction to just about all Facebook content by selecting one of these six sentiments as shown in the image below: Like, Love, Haha, Wow, Sad and Angry.

Figure 3.7: The six different reaction emojis on Facebook: Like, Love, Haha, Wow, Sad and Angry.

This change is significant and will help Facebook to better understand the emotions people had toward any given picture, video or status update. This will provide Facebook with the ability to improve their algorithm and offer more personalized content on users' News Feeds.

For companies who have Facebook Business Pages, new Facebook Reactions will provide an opportunity to obtain better feedback from their ideal clients as to what type of content they prefer to see.

In the future, Facebook advertisers will need to carefully follow their ads, as, for example, an ad with too many angry faces might indicate that you are targeting the wrong audience with your ad, and Facebook might limit showing it.

THREE SUGGESTED ACTION STEPS FROM CHAPTER 3:

Here are three suggested action steps related to the content of this Chapter. Try to complete these before moving to the next Chapter.

- Write down what you want to achieve with your personal Facebook profile and how it could support your business objectives.

- Spend at least 20 – 30 minutes visiting your Facebook privacy settings and Facebook security settings and configuring them correctly (strategies 23 and 24).

- Get familiar with Facebook Reactions and start to use different emojis when you want to express your opinion or emotion to different content you see on Facebook.

CHAPTER 4

Facebook Business Page Strategies

Most small and medium sized businesses need a Facebook Page for marketing and brand presence. However, many such businesses, which already utilize this service, struggle to do so properly, failing to use the right strategies for obtaining the results to best support the company's business objectives. The organic reach of a Facebook Page is diminishing these days, due largely in part to greater competition and oversaturation of the News Feed; your Facebook Page posts are being seeing by less people, requiring greater strategic effort to compensate.

Recently, Facebook paid advertising has become more popular to expand the marketing reach (covered in the next Chapter of this book). In this Chapter, you will learn simple yet powerful strategies, which may be implemented prior to paying for such advertising – tactics currently known and utilized by only a few companies – which may be applied to gain greater engagement and better results from Facebook business Pages.

31. Understand it's not about you, it's about them

It's not uncommon to see Facebook business Pages with a lot of content, but minimal audience comments, likes, or shares. Pages such as these have nearly zero impact on a business's marketing, and are often actually a waste of the company's time in maintaining. To effectively market your Facebook Page with these services, you need to post content which is interesting from your audience's point of view, not yours. In other words, it's all about what your

Page followers want to hear, not about what you want to say.

Here are few examples to better illustrate this point:

- Instead of giving a call to action to buy something, it's better to say something like, "Would you like to test this?"
- Instead of using the word "we" (as a company), use the word "you" (referring to the follower).
- Instead of talking about what is happening in your company, share posts related to what is happening in the lives of your followers. For example, during Christmas time you can share posts about the holidays; during summer holidays, you can share posts about those events.

To get yourself started, create a list of 10 different posts you can make using the above points. You will quickly see that there are many creative ways in which you can utilize the new focus in reaching your audience.

In addition, you may consider posting a survey to directly ask your customers what kind of content they might like to see on your Facebook page.

32. Take advantage of Facebook's mobile direction

According to the latest Nielsen statistics for the top smartphone applications of 2015, Facebook, YouTube, and the Facebook Messenger app were among the most commonly used. Facebook Messenger had 31% growth over 2014, and Facebook's apps generated more user engagement than Google's. This statistic is quite significant, essentially illustrating that Facebook dominates the mobile app market.

Smart business owners are already optimizing all their Facebook content for mobile devices. Most businesses, however, are far behind in this market, still believing that most of their customers visit Facebook only on desktop computers.

The following tips will help you to start optimizing your Facebook content for mobile devices:

- Make the text on your post easy to read by using short paragraphs and questions.
- Make sure photos, promotions and other text are all being seen correctly on a mobile device.
- When creating videos, make them short and mobile-friendly.
- Create a QR-code to enable customers to quickly follow your Facebook Page from their mobile devices.

Visit other Facebook Pages for businesses in your sector and analyze how well their posts and content are being viewed from your mobile device.

Download the latest version of the "**Facebook Pages Manager**" app, which allows you to quickly and easily post photos and updates, view and respond to messages, and view Page insights.

Figure 4.1: Screenshot from Facebook Pages Manager application.

If one of your employees manages or uploads content to your Facebook page, have them download this application and use it. Doing so will help to save time and to post content more effectively.

33. Avoid the mistakes your competitors are making

Imagine how powerful it would be to see the mistakes your competitors or other companies in your industry are making. Well, thanks to a variety of tools now available for download, that is now possible. Follow below, and see how to create powerful Facebook content plans and quickly achieve great results.

Here's how this works in practice, using the free online tool at *www.Likealyzer.com*:

- Let's suppose your business is an Italian restaurant in New York, and you want to learn from your competitors' mistakes.

- After doing some research, you find the Facebook Pages for three local competitors.

- Next, you go to *www.likealyzer.com* and type in the Facebook URL of each competitor page, and then click "enter" to start the analysis.

- Likealyzer.com will provide a specific list of actions that could improve each Facebook Page – actions which you can take yourself to improve your own restaurant's Facebook Page.

The following image shows the recommendations Likealyzer gives on how to improve the Page.

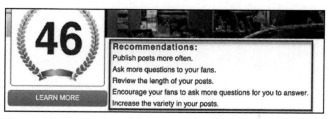

Figure 4.2: Screenshot of the recommendations provided by the Likealizer.com tool.

- I recommend printing out these results and recommendations, visiting and analyzing the competitors' Facebook pages, and then improving upon your own Facebook Page plan utilizing the site's recommendations.

- To get more creative ideas, you can do the same analysis for Facebook Pages from other industries and see what kinds of text and content they use.

34. Improve the engagement of your Facebook Page

Engagement is the most important keyword for Facebook Page administrators, and it's something businesses need to focus on more.

Here is a list of basic strategies to improve the engagement of your Facebook Page:

- Start your Facebook post with a question. If you are posting a picture, you can embed the question in the image. This helps people viewing your post on mobile devices to see the questions better.

- If you share a lengthy post, use a question at the end as well.

- Ask for your followers' opinions by posing two options and asking which one they like better.

- Answer each comment or question on your Page quickly; use a friendly and spontaneous tone.

- Have fun and use humor in your posts.

- Post statements that would be highly relevant for your followers. For example, a Facebook Page for tennis players could post an emotional statement about how one feels after playing a very good game (normally it's recommended to use a good image for this kind of post). Then you can ask people to share the post if they agree, or to comment if they disagree.

- Post more photos.

Aside from the above, you may consider creating more professional photos for your Page using online tools, such as *www.Canva.com*. Such free online tools often offer templates you can modify and change to fit your needs.

Spending some time and effort on creating beautiful visuals will significantly increase the likelihood of your fans sharing and engaging in your content.

Figure 4.3: Canva.com offers free templates you can use for Facebook posts.

After posting content by utilizing these tips for a few weeks, revisit your Facebook Page's insights and analyze which posts have helped you gain the most engagements. Learn from this and create more of these kinds of posts in the future.

In general, constantly trying to improve the engagement and interaction on your Page needs to be your key focus. The more engagement you can generate, the more reach Facebook will give you.

35. Drive local sales using specific promotions

Facebook is becoming increasingly more important for local companies who want to attract new local clients. A common mistake is to invite prospective customers to click on your Facebook Page's "Like" button and expect them to automatically buy your products.

Each company needs to consider what kinds of compelling offers they could give to their Facebook followers. The following are some examples that local companies could create for customers who link from Facebook.

- Restaurants could offer a free desert.
- Chiropractic professionals could offer a first session for free.
- Coaching professionals could offer a free report or first session.
- A lawyer could offer a free consultation.

Typically, I don't recommend offering discounts; they may decrease the perceived value of your product. However, companies that offer services as their product may offer a small test or sample, which can actually help to build trust and credibility. A large portion of prospective customers who accept such tests and samples stick around and become actual paying clients.

When creating a special offer for your Facebook fans, it's recommended to track both the number of contacts and the number of sales being generated via Facebook. Business owners need to track the following information in order to get a clear idea of how effective any Facebook promotion actually is:

- How many customers call you after seeing information about your special offer (make sure your employees ask the customers where they have seen the offer, if you run it on other social media sites simultaneously).

- How many customers contact you via the contact feature on the Facebook Page.
- How many customers send you an email.
- How many customers visit your business.

36. Share video content on your Facebook Page

The social media analytics company Quintly analyzed more than 80 million Facebook posts between June 2014 and June 2015. From this study they discovered that videos generate the most engagements over other types of Facebook content, including photos, status updates, and hyperlinks.

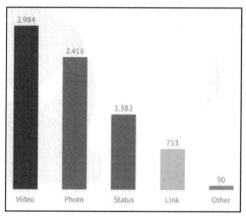

Figure 4.4: Chart: Average interactions per Facebook post type. Source: report by Quintly.com.

Several other studies have been conducted showing similar results. Video is still a new form of content and offers a different experience for Facebook users than photos, links, and status updates. And, in 2016, video content will only grow further as Facebook optimizes on these results. Companies using Facebook for advertising and marketing need to learn how to create relevant and interesting videos for their Pages to keep pace.

Facebook paid video advertising strategies will be covered in more detail later in this book, showing specific strategies for creating effective free video promotions on Facebook.

BASIC VIDEO MARKETING TIPS

The following are basic Facebook video marketing tips each company should take into consideration:

- Make videos that get to the point and have a lot of movement during the first three seconds. Most people see your video on their News Feed, and if the beginning of it is boring, they will not likely stop to watch it.
- Make sure the images in your video are big, as most people will view them on a mobile device.
- By default, videos on Facebook are muted, so you can use a call to action such as "Turn on your speakers" to encourage viewers to add audio.

Keep the videos short, generally between 15 – 60 seconds, depending on the content.

As an example, here is a screenshot image for the Facebook Page for Audi cars:

Figure 4.5: Audi's Facebook video channel can be found at www.facebook.com/audi/videos.

TYPES OF VIDEOS YOU SHOULD UPLOAD TO FACEBOOK

Today's consumers are more demanding, and have more options available to them than ever before. Video content helps companies to build trust and credibility with their prospective customers, and to stand out within the marketplace. The following are some example videos companies ought to create and share on their Facebook Pages:

- **Short video tutorials:** Your ideal clients love to learn useful content via quick video tutorials. Keep these video tutorials fast-moving and to the point, offering a call to action at the end for those who want to learn more.

- **Video testimonials and case-study videos:** Facebook is all about people, and when a consumer finds a video of someone sharing their experience with your product or service it greatly enhances their buying decision.

- **Slideshow videos:** These are the easiest form of videos because you only need a few images. An editor program can then combine these into a professional slideshow. My favorite iPhone application for creating slideshow videos is called "Replay" and can be found in the iOS app store.

- **Video presentations of products, the company, or employees:** Consumers normally want to see the people who work in a local store before visiting in person. Quick product and employee presentations, if professionally done and with minimal self-promotion, work well on the Facebook market.

SURPRISE YOUR AUDIENCE WITH CINEMAGRAPHS

According to Wikipedia: "Cinemagraphs are still photographs in which a minor and repeated movement occurs. Cinemagraphs, which are published in either animated GIF format or as video, can give the illusion that the viewer is watching a video." (source: www.wikipedia.org/wiki/Cinemagraph).

These are a new form of content that offer refreshing and surprising experiences for Facebook users who are used to viewing traditional photos or videos. Facebook now allows this media type to be uploaded, creating yet another new marketing tool at your disposal set to grow exponentially in the coming years.

37. Schedule your posts and save time

Time management is one of the key activities for busy business owners who want to run effective social media marketing. Most businesses struggle to post new content several times a day, but the content publication can be automated using Facebook's Schedule feature.

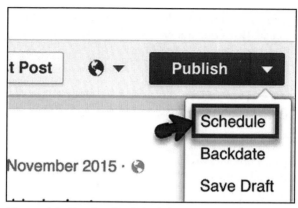

Figure 4.6: Facebook's Schedule option can be found by clicking on the dropdown arrow in the blue Publish button.

For instance, on Monday morning you can create all of the content for the whole week, and schedule the material to be posted on days and at times you want, automatically.

Although Facebook favors manually posting or at least using its own Schedule feature, there are several external tools which perform the same task. Some companies prefer to use third-party tools, and some of the most effective options are: *www.Bufferapp.com*, *www.hootsuite.com* and *www.meetedgar.com*.

38. Use specific language and words directed to your ideal customers

Your Facebook followers should have a pleasant user experience when reading your posts. This may in part be achieved by using language they can identify with.

A local restaurant should use local verbiage – words and phrases that people from the area can relate with. Perhaps this includes mixing in local humor and anecdotes. This kind of communication will provide memorable experiences for your Facebook followers, and make them feel more connected to your brand.

39. Encourage your customers to leave reviews, and position your company in the Facebook local search

According to several statistics, local clients use mobile searches in order to find consumer reviews and opinions. Google's local listings, also called Google My Business, along with Yelp.com, a similar search service, have long been the most crucial for ranking businesses in local searches. Facebook is, however, entering the market with its own such tool – **Facebook Professional Services**.

In 2016, **Facebook Professional** Services will launch to rank local businesses for its users - and placing strong emphasis on consumer reviews and opinions. Companies need to encourage their customers to leave comments on Facebook to increase the social proof and credibility of the business. You might have seen for yourself that after visiting a local business on Facebook you are encouraged to leave a review. Local companies should also provide complete and updated information on their Facebook Pages, including hours of operation, physical address, and contact information, as these are all shown in the Facebook Professional Services listings.

*Figure: 4.7: At www.facebook.com/services you can search
local businesses on Facebook.*

Presently, **Facebook Professional Services** has not yet
launched in all countries. Regardless, and particularly as it
becomes more widely available, it will surely play an
important role for companies who want to effectively use
Facebook for marketing – and who want to stand out
against competition as consumers consider their buying
options.

40. Improve your reach with specific News Feed targeting

If you have more than 5,000 fans or likes on your
Facebook Business Page, you can configure each post so
that it will target a certain audience.

Why is this a recommended practice? Targeting a certain
demographic that is more interested in the topic of your
content can improve engagement and is quite a
recommended practice for Facebook Pages with a large
following.

You can also target your content according to the language your fans speak. For example, on my own Facebook Page at *www.facebook.com/LasseVideo* (visit the page and click on "Like" if you have not done it yet), I have fans who speak English and others who speak Spanish. Thanks to this targeting option, I can offer relevant content for each of these groups.

To target your post, click on the target icon shown inFigure 4.8.

Figure 4.8: How to target specific News Feed audience when posting.

In the pop-up window you will see several targeting options like those shown inFigure 4.11:

- Interest.
- Age.
- Gender.
- Location.
- Language.

Figure 4.9: Facebook post targeting options.

Most Facebook Page administrators are unaware of this option, and I highly recommend that you become familiar with it. Each time I have used it, it has generated better results than posting to all of my Facebook fans.

THREE SUGGESTED ACTION STEPS FROM CHAPTER 4:

Here are three suggested action steps related to the content of this Chapter. Try to complete these before moving to the next Chapter.

- Download the latest version of the app "Facebook Pages Manager" and get familiar with all the functionalities it has and how you can use it to share new content on your Facebook Page

- Review the tips related to how to increase the engagement of your Facebook page shared in strategy 34. Create a list of at least five strategies you will use on your Facebook Page.

- Make a list of different videos you could create and share on your Facebook page following the tips shared in strategy 36.

CHAPTER 5

Basic Facebook Advertising Strategies

According to Facebook's official statistics, the social media giant has more than 1.4 billion active users and over 900 million visits every day. The Facebook advertising platform is therefore one of most powerful marketing tools available for businesses today. However, many business owners find it confusing or frustrating to start using the available tools, limiting their potential reach.

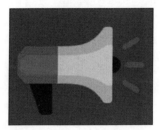

Figure 5.1: Facebook advertising.

In this Chapter, you will learn step-by-step how to get started with Facebook advertising's most prevalent tools. Other more advanced advertising products, like Facebook video marketing, is covered in various other Chapters of this book.

41. Uncover basic Facebook advertising vocabulary

If you are just getting started with Facebook advertising, you might come across various new terms that you've never heard before. To benefit from the strategies outlined throughout this book, it's important that you first understand some of the key terminology used in the industry.

- **Ad Account:** Everything related to your advertising activity is in your ad account: ads, campaigns, billing information, reports, etc. If you manage Facebook ads for a company, they can give you access to their ad account.

- **Ads Manager:** This is where you create new ads or analyze your previous ads. When running Facebook campaigns, it's recommended that you review Ads Manager daily. Ads Manager can be found at: *www.facebook.com/ads/manage*.

- **Bidding:** Facebook allows you to use either manual or automatic bidding when setting up your campaigns. Often for new users, automatic bidding is easier to use and so may generate better results. However, everything is case specific and so you should test both options to see which works better for you.

- **Campaign:** In order to organize all of your ads, Facebook has created the following structure: Campaign > Ad Set > Ad. Each campaign can have several Ad Sets, and each Ad Set may have several Ads.

- **Campaign Budget: This is the amount of money you are willing to spend** on each of your campaigns. You can run several campaigns simultaneously and modify the budget as you go.

- **Conversions:** This is related to actions customers have completed, i.e., products purchased or signups for newsletters.

- **Cost per lead (CPL):** Cost of the leads generated with Facebook advertising. This is one of the most important metrics you need to track and follow.

- **Cost per click (CPC):** The average cost of the clicks generated by Facebook advertising.

- **CPM (Cost per 1,000 Impressions):** The average cost per 1,000 impressions on your Facebook ad.

- **Click-through rate (CTR):** The number of clicks your ad generated divided by the number of impressions. The more effective the ad, the higher the CTR you will normally have.

- **Frequency:** The average number of times your ad is being shown to each Facebook user.

- **Objective:** Each Facebook ad should have a specific objective, such as website visits, website conversions, or improved engagement with your Facebook posts.

- **Page engagement:** Number of actions related to your page's posts as a result of your ad.

- **Reach:** Number of people who see your Facebook advertisement.

- **Relevance Score:** Score ranging from 1 – 10 indicating how relevant your ad is to your audience.

- **Reports:** Summaries of important data and metrics related to your Facebook advertising campaign, found at _www.facebook.com/ads/manager_.

The above is not an exhaustive list; however, it provides some fundamental terminology necessary to understand before creating or improving your Facebook ad campaigns.

42. Discover basic Facebook advertising concepts

Before beginning with ad creation, let's first try to understand the overall strategy behind this activity. Facebook advertising allows you to reach your ideal clients; however, this is a gradual process of testing various options, and results cannot be expected immediately.

WHERE FACEBOOK CAN SHOW YOUR AD

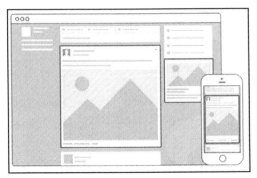

Figure: 5.2: Facebook ad placement (Image source:
www.facebook.com/business/ads-guide).

Currently, Facebook offers to show your ad in three different locations:

- **News Feed:** On the default and primary Facebook window, where you see all of the stories and News Feeds (on desktop).
- **Right-hand column:** On the right-hand side column (on desktop).
- **On a mobile News Feed:** On a central area when visiting Facebook on your mobile device.

For most markets, placement on the News Feed is usually the most effective. The ad images can be bigger, and you can include more text. To show your ads in the News Feed, a Facebook page is required.

FOUR ELEMENTS OF AN EFFECTIVE FACEBOOK ADVERTISING CAMPAIGN

The following four elements are crucial to understand if you want great and effective Facebook advertising campaigns:

- **Compelling offer:** Offer something your ideal clients really want and that are valuable to them.
- **Targeted audience:** Try to find your ideal clients using Facebook advanced targeting options.
- **Attractive ad image:** Try to make your advertising image relevant and interesting to your target audience.
- **Specific landing page:** Send the traffic to a page which is relevant and highly related to your offer, not just to your main website.

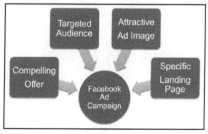

Figure 5.3: Four elements of an effective Facebook Advertising Campaign.

A bit later in this Chapter we will cover more in depth each of these elements.

FOUR THINGS YOU NEED TO KNOW BEFORE YOU START

What is your objective or specific product you want to promote? Decide whether you want to generate more visits to your website, more email sign-ups, or promote some specific offer. Never use Facebook just to promote your main website, but rather to create more specific promotional targeting for your most profitable product.

What is your budget? Each campaign has its own separate budget establishing the maximum amount you will spend. I recommend beginning small to test your advertising progress while you find what works best for your needs.

What is the profit margin of your product? How much profit will each sale generate for you versus the costs expended in doing so? Try to carefully analyze what your profit margin is for each product you promote.

How much are you willing to pay in order to obtain new clients? Carefully calculate your profit margin as compared to how much (or how much more) you are willing to spend against that margin.

Facebook allows you to begin budgeting with as little as $5. You can also pause or end your campaign at any time.

43. Learn from the most common Facebook advertising mistakes and how to avoid them – Part I

Understanding the most common pitfalls made by others will help you to avoid them yourself. Before discovering the step-by-step actions involved in creating a profitable Facebook ad campaign, review some of the following problematic examples:

- **Not having patience:** So many business owners begin Facebook campaigns expecting immediate results. The necessary delays cause frustration, creating even less incentive to learn how to market the product successfully. It's important that you stay patient and always try to learn something new.

- Facebook advertising is a world of its own, offering surprises and frustrations. But, you will achieve success if you patiently and carefully follow all the strategies provided in this book. Accept the fact that not everything will be perfect, and that successful campaigning is an ongoing learning experience.

- **Not having clear objectives:** Every campaign needs a specific business objective. The most common are getting more website clicks, getting more engagement for your Facebook posts, or generating more website conversions. Don't start Facebook advertising before you have a clear objective.

- **"Set it and forget it" mentality:** You need to visit your Facebook reports every day to analyze the results and make improvements. Never start a campaign and then leave it on its own without following the results. Doing so will almost always result in losing money.

- **Just creating one ad:** Get into the habit of always creating several ads, rather than just one. Having multiple ads helps you to test different ad images, and to target different audiences - allowing you to learn what works, what doesn't, and later allocating your budget more effectively.

- **Boosting a post:** Below every post is a button called "Boost Post." I recommend against using this feature as you're restricted from selecting the best targeting options and other features which make your ad most effective. Boosting posts every now and then is fine, but do so from your Facebook Ad Creation tool: *www.facebook.com/ads/create*.

Figure 5.4: Boost Post button.

44. Learn from the most common Facebook advertising mistakes and how to avoid them – Part II

Interested in learning some more common mistakes to avoid? The below errors are examples first-time advertisers most often commit on Facebook.

- **Not testing different images:** Almost 80% of your Facebook ad's success is tied to how good of an image you use. It's not easy to know to what kind of image your target audience will respond best. Therefore, try placing two or three images in each ad. Facebook will automatically show each image and you will easily see which generated the best results. Delete the images that don't work, and allocate more of your budget to those images that work best.

- **"20% Text Rule" on ad images:** Your Facebook ad image can have a short call to action or question, but Facebook does not allow you to use more than 20% of the space as text. To save time and effort, always use this free Facebook tool to see if your image has more than 20% text: www.facebook.com/ads/tools/text_overlay.

- **Thinking that everyone on Facebook is your client:** Facebook ad targeting options allow extremely specific targeting, therefore giving an opportunity to pay less for effectiveness. A common mistake is not using the Facebook ad targeting options, and instead trying to reach everyone on Facebook, regardless of audience. The ad targeting options are covered in more detail later in this Chapter of the book.

- **Not dedicating time to learn from your results:** Each day you ought to visit Facebook reports to analyze metrics, see which ads work, and which don't. The most essential metrics are covered at the end of this Chapter. Try to set aside time to analyze the results each day, and to learn from the various parts reported.

- **Not familiarizing yourself with Facebook's advertising policies:** Failing to adhere to Facebook's advertising policies can result in being banned from the service, and all of your content being deleted from the servers. Take the time to carefully read through the various policies, understand what it is you're agreeing to by using the service, and what you can and cannot do. The advertising policies can be found at *www.facebook.com/policies/ads.*

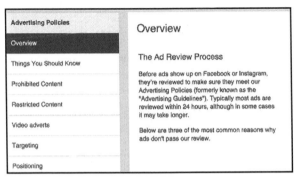

Figure: 5.5: Screenshot of Facebook's advertising policies

45. Create a compelling offer for your ad

Let's now cover the first element of an effective Facebook marketing campaign - your offer. As mentioned before, avoid creating generic campaigns without any specific offer or that just promote the name of your business. Those typically will not generate the results you are after.

The following are some examples of compelling offers different businesses might create:

- **Free trial:** A local gym or health club could promote a free trial, incentivizing people to test their facilities. A certain percentage of the people who use a free trial will sign up for a paid membership.

- **Free newsletter sign-up:** Companies which promote a service can offer a free newsletter. Providing

CHAPTER 5 – Basic Facebook Advertising Strategies

valuable information attached to your brand is a proper way of increasing your audience and increasing name recognition.

- **Special bonus:** Event organizers, music groups, or public speakers might offer a special bonus if people sign up for their event before a certain date. Restaurants or hotels can also use this by offering a free dessert or extra meal when a group of people come to eat.

- **Free session:** Coaches or business consultants can offer a first evaluation session for free. This is normally a quick session and also allows the coach to evaluate whether the client is a good fit for the service.

- **Free training:** Online marketers or business professionals can offer a free online seminar or webinar to teach something valuable, attaching an offer for the paid product at the end of the lesson.

The above offers are merely examples; the possibilities are limitless.

Promoting a discount may lower the perceived value of a product, later making it more difficult to sell at the normal price. However, discounts can still be a valuable tool at your disposal if you know your profit margin and calculate the overall return on investment from your campaign.

The general Facebook audience you are targeting doesn't yet know or trust you, so the main purpose of having a compelling offer is to build credibility. Once that has been established, it then becomes easier to conduct your actual business.

46. Select the correct target audience for your ad

Knowing your target audience is probably the most essential element of a successful Facebook ad campaign. No other platform allows you to target as precisely as Facebook, so it's worth taking the time to learn how. The better your targeting, the more people who will respond to your ad, and the less you will pay. Successful targeting makes for a higher return on profit.

Facebook has a free audience creation tool, found at *www.facebook.com/ads/create*. Just select the objective for your campaign and go to the next page (you can use this without creating your campaign). On the next page you should see the audience tool.

When creating your first audience, try to identify the age, gender, and interests of your ideal customer. Later, you can make these criteria more specific. Ideally, you would create several different audiences for each campaign and analyze which one responds most to your ad.

Here is an example audience, targeting for an e-commerce store selling hiking equipment in the United States.

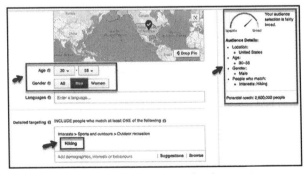

Figure 5.6: Example of Facebook targeting.

Targeting for an audience interested in hiking and living in the United States. This audience has been selected with the following criteria:

Geographical region: United States
Age: 30 – 55
Gender: Men
Interest: Hiking

As you can see from the Figure 5.6, Facebook states that the audience size is 2.6 million. This is a bit too broad for our purposes.

To narrow your audience, further limit the geographic scope to where hiking is most popular (earlier in the book I shared how you can find this by using Google Trends). You may also narrow the consumer's age, or find more specific interests to reach avid hikers. Maybe there is a hiking magazine you can target or an influential hiker with a large following.

This was just a quick and simple example using basic demographic data. However, Facebook allows a number of additional targeting parameters, such as: work place, marital status, behavior, and travel habits.

Try to create at least three different targeting options to test and see which will work best for your business and goals. Once you find a target that generated optimal results, allocate more of your budget to that specific campaign. You can also consider advanced targeting options, details for which are covered in the next Chapter of this book.

EXPERT OPINION – Charles Kirkland

"Most advertisers make the mistake of not taking advantage of all the targeting options Facebook offers. For example, knowing if your ideal audience uses Android phones or iPhones makes all the difference in the world.

Facebook allows us to filter our targeting according to which phone the user has, and if you are targeting a business user who carries an iPhone 3, that person is totally different from an iPhone 6 user who always buys the latest technology and probably has more disposable income and is ready to spend it."

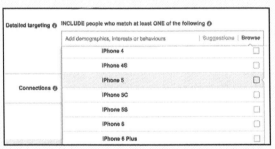

Figure 5.7: Example of how to target different iPhone users on Facebook

47. Use effective ad images on Facebook

The first rule for choosing an image for your ad is to make it relevant and interesting to your target audience. Use something that captivates and entertains, while staying appropriate to the nature of the business. Color also matters. Below are two images which contrast how this can work in practice. The yellow ad on the left catches the eye; the white ad to the right gets glanced over. As a general rule, avoid using white and blue – the colors of

Facebook – as your content might disappear into the backdrop.

Figure 5.8: Two examples of Facebook advertisements.

It's also recommended that you use the same images from your landing page (the first page on your website where people who see your ad go after clicking on the image). Additionally, utilizing people's faces will create more connection to your product or service, more clicks, and overall greater response - especially if the person in the ad is a knownFigure in the business or industry, or generally known by the target audience.

Want to learn from other businesses' ads? Beginning now, take screenshots of any Facebook ads that catch your attention; save the ads in a specific folder for later review, including why they caught your attention and how you might use that information for your own content. Doing this myself for the last 3 years has helped me to see successful patterns companies use in their ad images.

A great recourse is AdEpresso's Facebook Ads Gallery, found online at *https://adespresso.com/academy/ads-examples.* Currently, this is the biggest ad gallery available. It offers ads across different industries and with different ad objectives.

Figure: 5.9: The Facebook Ads Gallery by AdEspresso.

I recommend spending at least 30 minutes analyzing different ads with this tool, which you can later reference when planning your first campaign.

The easiest tool for beginning with your ad creation is Canva, offering free templates for use at: *www.canva.com/create/social-media-graphics*.

48. Use an effective landing page for your Facebook ads

A landing page – the website to which traffic is directed after clicking an ad – is another aspect of marketing often overlooked in the process. Every one of your ad campaigns should link to a landing page which is relevant to your ad. If your ad offered a promise, make sure that the necessary information is provided on (or easily found after first landing on) that page.

It may be necessary or appropriate to create a separate landing page specific to the audience you have selected (and which delivers on the promise made in your ad). Avoid sending traffic directly to your website's homepage.

LeadPages is recommended software to help novices quickly create mobile landing pages; no coding or website development experience is needed. I have personally used

LeadPages for several years, and highly recommend it to all small businesses and professionals who want to create successful landing pages.

Figure 5.10: Example landing pages template in LeadPages.

LeadPages offers several different templates for businesses which are easy to customize. You can find it at *www.leadpages.net*. Other similar landing page services include *www.unbounce.com* and *www.instapage.com*.

49. Analyze Facebook advertising metrics and results

"What gets measured gets improved." This is a famous quote by management consultant Peter Drucker, and holds very true with our discussion. As mentioned before, many businesses don't spend enough time and effort understanding how their campaigns could be improved. However, measuring and learning from your performance is a vital part of Facebook advertising.

Some of the metrics you want to analyze in each campaign include:

- **Spend:** How much money has been spent?
- **Clicks:** How many clicks have been generated?
- **Cost per click or CPC:** What is the cost of each click?
- **Click-through rate (CTR):** The higher the CTR, the better your ad is working.

Your advertising reports can be found at *www.facebook.com/ads/manager*. As seen in the image below, you can collect basic information like: spent in the last 7 days, results, reach, and cost. By clicking on the name of each campaign you will be shown a more detailed breakdown of the metrics.

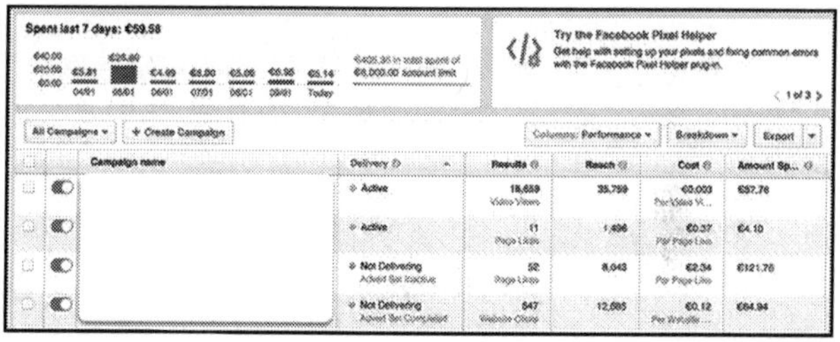

Figure 5.11: Example view of advertising reports from inside Facebook Ads Manager.

Using one of your campaigns, test several different audiences and ad images. Facebook shows the results being generated from which you can more effectively allocate your budget.

Facebook reports also indicate which part of your target audience responds best to your ads. In the image below, you can see that people ages 35 – 44 years old were most responsive to this ad. The conclusion would be to target only this segment in the next campaign; typically, this will generate lower click cost and better return on investment.

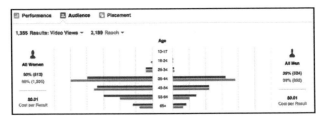

Figure 5.12: Facebook ad results illustrated according to the age and gender of the audience.

According to Facebook, the ad performance metrics are updated in real time. So, it's advisable to review them several times a day and track their status.

There are several advanced options to better measure and improve the effectiveness of your campaign, but you can start by following the basic tips shared in this Chapter.

50. Learn from frequently asked Facebook advertising questions

Excited to start your first campaign and test these tips in real life? Before you do, here are some common questions and answers asked by my consulting students.

What kind of text do you recommend using in Facebook ads?

- Mention your target audience in the first sentence: For instance: *Are you a dog lover who wants to...*

- **Questions:** Starting with a question gets people's attention and typically generates good results. For example: *Do you want to get more* _____?

- **Calls to action:** If you use a short paragraph, try to end it with a short call to action. *For example, click here to* _____.

- **Testimonial:** You can put a short customer experience in quotation marks so users understand it's someone's opinion of your product

What is the size of the Facebook ad images?

News Feed ads: 1,200 x 628 pixels.
Right column image size: 254 x 133 pixels.
Carousel ads: 600 x 600 pixels (Carousel ads will be explained in the next Chapter).

Can I establish a limit for my Facebook advertising account?

Yes, you can set a specific limit for your advertising account as a whole, and also individually for each campaign. When creating your ad you are asked to select either a daily budget or a lifetime budget. Daily budgets have always worked better for me, and it's what I recommend to my clients.

How long can my ads run effectively?

The term *delivery fatigue* refers to when your audience starts to see the same ad too many times; when this happens, Facebook will start to limit its reach. If your News Feed ads keep getting positive comments and likes, on the other hand, then Facebook may keep running it longer.

To continue after your ads become stale, you can renew the same campaign but with a different target audience or image.

Should I respond to people's comments on my ads?

Of course! The more engagement your ads generate (comments, likes, or shares), the better your ads work. Normally, this also helps you to pay less. You should always respond to comments quickly and encourage people to ask more questions.

How can I contact someone on Facebook's advertising support team?

You can contact them using email support provided on this page:
www.facebook.com/business/contact-us.

What are some Facebook advertising resources you recommend to be followed?

Two of the best sites sharing a lot of useful tips are Jon Loomer's blog at *www.jonloomer.com*, and AdEspresso's blog at adespresso.com/academy/blog.

THREE SUGGESTED ACTION STEPS FROM CHAPTER 5:

Here are three suggested action steps related to the content of this Chapter. Try to complete these before moving to the next Chapter.

- Review and learn the basic Facebook advertising vocabulary shared in strategy 41, as it is important to know these terms before starting your ad campaigns.

- Make a list of what your first Facebook ads might be and write down what could be the different elements like: your offer, your targeting, your ad image and your landing page (strategy 42).

- Carefully study strategy 46 and learn how Facebook ad targeting works. Visit *www.facebook.com/ads/create* and create your first ad targeting without starting the campaign.

CHAPTER 6

Advanced Facebook Advertising Strategies

In this Chapter, you will find additional tips and strategies for advertising on Facebook. Although the word *"advanced"* is in the name of the Chapter, don't be scared if you are just getting started. Most of these techniques are quite simple to implement and the word "advanced" is simply used to differentiate them from the basic strategies covered in the previous Chapter.

All in all, I recommend applying each of these strategies, as they can make a significant difference in your advertising results when implemented correctly.

51. Sign up with Facebook Business Manager

If you run Facebook campaigns for clients or use more than one advertising account on Facebook, you should consider signing up with Facebook Business Manager. Business Manager is a more secure way of handling your Pages and advertising accounts, and it enables you to give ad account access to your employees.

The central interface allows you to easily and quickly change your billing details or other crucial information related to your Facebook advertising campaigns. If you ever have problems with your Facebook ads and want to contact Facebook ad support, they will usually appreciate it if you have access to Business Manager, as this will give them a more accurate view of your business.

You can create your account on Facebook Business Manager here: *https://business.facebook.com*.

52. Manage your Facebook advertising campaigns on-the-go with Facebook Ads Manager mobile application

This particular tip is not just an advanced strategy, but is rather a recommendation that all advertisers should follow. Facebook Ads Manager lets all advertisers enjoy these benefits:

- Receive notifications regarding your campaigns.
- Quickly modify or make changes to your campaigns.
- Keep track of your advertising spending.
- Create new ads or stop the ads that are not effective.
- View and analyze insights.

Figure 6.1: Facebook Ads Manager – Image credit: iTunes store.

The Facebook Ads Manager application can be downloaded here:

Apple App Store link:
https://itunes.apple.com/us/app/facebook-ads-manager/id964397083

Google Play Store link:
https://play.google.com/store/apps/details?id=com.facebo ok.adsmanager

53. Become familiar with Facebook Power Editor

Facebook Power Editor serves as an advanced ad creation tool, featuring a full range of useful functions that can help you to take advantage of all the opportunities offered by Facebook advertising components. Power Editor might feel time-consuming when you first start using it, but it will ultimately allow you to run your campaigns more effectively once you get used to it.

This tool is designed for advertisers who wish to create many Facebook ad campaigns simultaneously (or "at scale"), and the following items include just a few of its benefits:

- More options for the number of characters your ad can use. Typical News Feed ads are limited to 90 characters. Power Editor increases these limits.
- Ability to create an unpublished page post: Basically, this enables you to create News Feed ads that look like a post, without having them show up on your Facebook feed. This gives you an opportunity to test several ad variations without annoying your current Facebook fans.
- More options to quickly create several campaigns or ad sets, testing different ad variables.
- Ability to use bulk editing, enabling you to modify your ads faster and save time.
- Ability to duplicate ads, ad sets, and campaigns.

There are a number of other benefits to the Power Editor function, and as with any tool, some time may be needed to discover all of its powerful features.

You can start using Facebook Power Editor at: *www.facebook.com/ads/manage/powereditor*. Make sure you are on a Chrome web browser, since it does not work with other browsers.

54. Take advantage of local advertising opportunities on Facebook

Facebook provides businesses with many new opportunities and tools to help promote their companies locally. Facebook seems to have a special interest in attracting companies to advertise with them in their local markets. When creating an ad on Facebook and using the audience-targeting options shared earlier, you can add an extra layer of targeting, reaching only Facebook users within a specific distance of your business.

This advertising option is extremely powerful, but only a few local businesses really take advantage of it. Suppose you want to open a new yoga studio in Manhattan, New York, located in the ZIP code 10018. Creating your target audience is simple: Type in the ZIP code and Facebook will limit the reach of your ad to customers located within that area.

You can see an example of this type of targeting below. Notice that this ad would reach 6,300 people between 20 – 50 years of age who like yoga and are located in the ZIP code 10018. Can you imagine the effect this type of advertising could have for your local business?

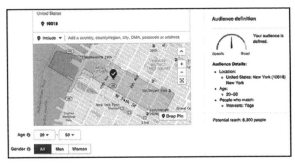

Figure 6.2: Example of how to target a local audience with Facebook Ads.

Local targeting by Facebook used to work only in the United States, but is now available in most countries. The testing I have done with it has generated great results.

FACEBOOK LOCAL AWARENESS ADS

Most Facebook ad objectives (like boosting a post, generating more website visits, etc.) allow you to use the local targeting feature, but Facebook has launched Local Awareness Ads, which come with specific calls to action, like getting directions or calling the business directly.

Figure 6.3: Different calls to action you can select with Local Awareness Ads.

The only disadvantage to using Local Awareness Ads is that at the time of writing this book, Facebook does not allow you to use them with interested targeting (for example, Chinese restaurants cannot target people who like Chinese food, as they can with other ad options).

To start using Local Awareness Ads, select the "*Reach people near your business*" option when you choose the objective of your campaign at *www.facebook.com/ads/create.*

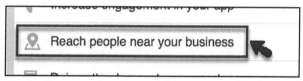

Figure 6.4: Ad objective you need to select when creating Local Awareness Ads.

55. Tap into the power of Facebook Remarketing

Has this ever happened to you: You are looking at a specific product on Amazon.com and a few moments later when visiting Facebook, you see an ad for that same product you just viewed on Amazon? That is how remarketing works. These kinds of ads used to be quite expensive and complicated to conduct, but today, you can start using them for free by following a few simple steps.

Currently, when remarketing is done properly, it is probably the fastest way that online businesses or business owners can improve the return on their investment through Facebook marketing.

HOW TO START FACEBOOK REMARKETING

To get started, you can install a Facebook pixel code on your website, which will begin to track all of your website visitors, allowing you to later target them with your ads. This code is installed once on your main website, but lets you create audiences according to different parameters (for example, people who visited a certain page on your website, but did not make a purchase, etc.).

You can find the Facebook pixel code on Ads Manager at *www.facebook.com/ads/manager/pixel/facebook_pixel* and install it yourself or have your webmaster install it for you on your website.

People visiting your website will be in your audience during a maximum of 180 days from the day they first visit your site, and it's recommended that you install this code as soon as possible, even though you may not start advertising for several weeks, since it will help to build your potential audience.

56. Use Facebook Custom Audiences

Most of the time when someone sees your ad on Facebook, they don't know you or trust you yet. Building trust and credibility is one of the main marketing objectives you'll need to consider before expecting a potential customer to make a purchase decision.

But what if you could market to people who already know you and your business? With Facebook Custom Audiences, you can show ads to people who are on your email list or who have been your clients before. Typically, this type of audience is much more responsive to your ads, since they are already familiar with you and your business.

When starting a new advertising campaign, I always try to use a Custom Audience if possible, since doing so generates much better results than just using normal Facebook targeting.

HOW TO CREATE A CUSTOM AUDIENCE ON FACEBOOK

To start, you simply need to export customer data (such as email addresses) from your company database or CRM and upload them to Facebook. This process is totally legal and is done in a privacy-safe manner.

Inside your Ads Manager, you have audiences sections, found at
www.facebook.com/ads/manager/audiences/manage,
where you can create the first audience by clicking on "Create Audience" and then selecting "Custom Audience."

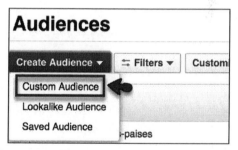

Figure 6.5: Where to create a Custom Audience.

Next, click on *"Customer List"* and upload your customer list, which can include email addresses or phone numbers. Customer lists can also be copied and pasted or imported from MailChimp, if you happen to use that service provider.

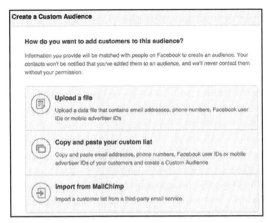

Figure 6.6: Screenshot of how to create a Custom Audience on Facebook.

Remember, you can only import people who are already on your email list or have bought something from you. When conducting this for the first time, it's advisable to carefully read the terms of service related to Custom Audiences, which can be found at *www.facebook.com/ads/manage/customaudiences/tos.php.*

57. Expand your reach with Facebook's Lookalike Audience

Once you have created different Custom Audiences, Facebook recommends that you create a Lookalike Audience. Basically, Facebook will create the "Lookalike Audience" by analyzing the behavior, relevant demographic data, and several other indicators, and using that information to create a new audience that is very similar to your original audience.

This is yet another highly effective method of creating a new and more targeted audience that will typically respond better to your ads. As a rule of thumb, you should try to create as many Custom Audiences and Lookalike Audiences as possible, as they can give you great leverage and options for running effective campaigns.

HOW TO CREATE A LOOKALIKE AUDIENCE

In the same area where you create Custom Audiences, a new Lookalike Audience can be created by clicking on "*Create Audience*" and then selecting "*Lookalike Audience*." You can use these three sources to create your Lookalike Audience:

- Custom Audience.
- Conversion-Tracking Pixel.
- Facebook Business Page.

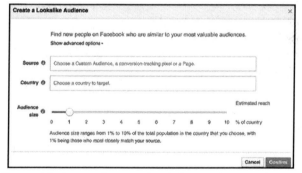

Figure 6.7: Screen that Facebook shows when you create a Lookalike Audience.

The minimum audience that can be used to create a Lookalike Audience is 100 people, but it's recommended that you have a list of at least 150 people to start with. All of the audiences you create can be found in the Audience sections of your Ads Manager at

www.facebook.com/ads/manager/audiences/manage.
When creating an ad, you can use these as a base audience
and then further narrow the audience by age, gender, or
interest.

58. Improve your ad performance by using Carousel Ads

Seeing the same type of ad over and over again on
Facebook will ultimately generate *"banner blindness,"* a
term used to describe a phenomenon where a user
consciously or subconsciously ignores ads. Facebook's
new ad format, Carousel Ads, offers a totally new
experience to the users and catches their attention by
showing a different kind of ad than they are used to.

Figure 6.8: Two examples of Carousel Ads.

Carousel Ads are also referred to as multi-product ads,
since you can show 3–5 images in one ad unit, with each
product having its own description.

Carousel Ads work perfectly for e-commerce stores that
do remarketing by showing product images to clients who
have just visited their online store. In general, all
businesses should test these kinds of ads. They are not that

widely used yet and generate more engagement and a better click-through rate than traditional Facebook ads.

59. Grow your email list with Facebook Lead Ads

Excited to grow your email list with Facebook advertising? The new Facebook Leads Ads option offers a great lead generation opportunity that will enable you to quickly generate a lot of email subscribers. At the time of writing this book, Facebook Lead Ads are only for mobile ads, but they will later be available for Facebook video ads and traditional desktop ads as well.

Marketers have long been using Facebook advertising to generate newsletter or webinar sign-ups. According to internal data at Facebook, it takes 38.5% longer to fill out forms on a mobile platform than on a desktop. This is mainly because most landing pages are not mobile-optimized, meaning that users end up disliking their experience filling out forms when using a mobile phone.

The following are some of the benefits of using Facebook Lead Ads for users:

Users have no need to visit a landing page to sign up, but can sign up right in the mobile app.

- Users have no need to write their contact information, since information is pre-populated by Facebook (users can change or modify their contact information if needed).

- The whole process is very quick, since there is no need to visit a website and wait for it to load.

- After signing up, the user can stay on Facebook, allowing them to continue what they were doing before.

- The process respects the privacy of users and companies cannot re-sell the lead information to third-party companies.

Here are the benefits of Facebook Lead Ads for companies:

- Lead Ads can be used for multiple-lead generation purposes, like generating pre-orders, event registrations, product testing, etc.
- Specific forms can be created for each campaign. For example, you can also include a short question that users need to respond to.
- It's quite likely that the leads generated from Facebook Lead Ads are of high quality, since people are signing up with their Facebook email, which is usually their main email, while on a traditional landing page email form, some people sign up with dummy emails.
- The process can be connected with some CRM (customer relationship management) solutions like Salesforce, Marketing Cloud, Driftrock, Marketo, and Maropost. This allows you to follow up with the leads, further nurturing the relationship with them and building trust and credibility.

In the image below, you can see the results of my recent Lead Ads campaign, which generated the following results:

- Total number of leads: 224
- Cost for each lead: $0.47
- Amount spent: $105.13

This campaign was generated for an audience in Mexico, where the cost per lead is traditionally a bit lower than in the United States or Western European countries, due to less competition.

Figure 6.9: Example results of Facebook Lead Ads campaign.

When creating your first Lead Ads campaign, make sure you have an email follow-up sequence that reminds the leads where they signed up. Most users quickly sign up on their mobile devices and later forget about it, but if you have a clear follow-up campaign, it will help tremendously.

60. Learn from frequently asked questions related to advanced Facebook advertising strategies

Here are some frequently asked questions that my consulting clients ask:

You have mentioned a lot of different Facebook advertising options, but would you recommend advertising that is targeted toward getting more Facebook Page Likes (Facebook fans)?

For most businesses, the value of a Facebook fan is getting lower (especially if you don't implement the strategies mentioned earlier on how to improve engagement) and therefore, I would only spend a small portion of your advertising budget toward acquiring new fans.

Local businesses are an exception and can create effective campaigns to increase their Facebook fans by targeting people who are interested in their product and are located geographically close to them. For example, an Italian restaurant could target people within 2 miles of their location and who like Italian food. For most other businesses, it's more beneficial to increase their email list (Facebook Lead Ads) than Facebook Likes.

I will not start remarketing yet, but should I still install the Facebook remarketing pixel on my sites?

Absolutely! One of the benefits of doing this is that it will start to create your audience now and you can target that audience whenever you are ready. Ideally, you should insert the Facebook pixel into as many websites as possible, as it will allow you to use the power of remarketing more effectively.

I have heard of Facebook Dynamic Product Ads. What are they exactly?

Dynamic Product Ads allow you to upload your product catalogue, including product name, description, landing page URL, etc., to Facebook and automatically show a large number of relevant ads to online shoppers without the need for creating each ad separately.

You can use Dynamic Product Ads on Facebook Power Editor, and they work on both desktop and mobile devices.

There are so many different ad options, how do I know which one to choose?

First, define your advertising objective and then analyze which type of ad would be the most suitable for you. For example, if you are a local business, you should start with Facebook Local Ads. If you have multiple products on sale, Carousel Ads might work great for you. Little by little, try to become familiar with all of the different ad products that Facebook offers, as they can all help you to reach and engage with your ideal clients.

I tested Facebook Lead Ads, but some leads were unresponsive and of low quality.

Here are three important recommendations:

- Try to improve your targeting and make sure you audience is interested in whatever you are offering.

- Make sure your call to action on the Lead Ad is clear, so the user knows what exactly he or she is getting.

- Make sure you follow up with your leads correctly, reminding them about why they signed up and who they can contact, if needed.

THREE SUGGESTED ACTION STEPS FROM CHAPTER 6:

Here are three suggested action steps related to the content of this Chapter. Try to complete these before moving to the next Chapter.

- Sign up with Facebook Business Manager (strategy 51), as it has several benefits for your advertising activities.

- Get familiar with the advanced Facebook advertising concepts of Facebook Remarketing (strategy 55) and Facebook Custom Audiences (strategy 56). Currently they are the most powerful features Facebook offers and are well worth the time you spend learning them.

- Test how Facebook Carousel Ads work (strategy 58), as you can achieve surprisingly good results with them compared to other types of ads.

CHAPTER 7

Facebook Video Marketing Strategies

Personally, I consider Facebook video advertising to be one of the greatest marketing and advertising opportunities of 2016 and 2017. I have always been fascinated by the impact of video marketing (you can learn more from the book *101 Video Marketing Tips and Strategies for Small Businesses[1]*), and now Facebook offers video advertising opportunities which can generate extremely beneficial results for your company.

61. Discover why Facebook video advertising is such a big opportunity for your business

There are a wide range of reasons why video advertising is a growing trend. Here are just few of the main reasons.

Movement catches people's attention

As mentioned several times before in this book, people's attention spans are getting shorter all the time, and it is becoming more difficult to catch their attention with just traditional Facebook content like photos and status updates. Video offers something new, different and impactful, and therefore video content has a greater chance of getting noticed.

---

[1] http://www.amazon.com/dp/1494770024

Video builds trust and credibility

Although videos used for ads are quite short, they still help to generate trust and credibility toward your company. The use of video is growing rapidly on the Internet, and consumers prefer to view video content before deciding whether to make a purchase.

Statistics don't lie – Facebook video is huge

According to official statistics from Facebook, the social network has 8 billion daily video views and some argue more videos are being viewed on Facebook than on YouTube. This trend is only going to grow even more in the future.

Facebook video ads offer powerful options for advertising

An additional reason for using Facebook video ads is the fact that currently Facebook's advertising platform is the easiest for small businesses to start with and offers powerful features that can be used with the video ads, such as local targeting.

62. Avoid common Facebook video advertising mistakes

Starting Facebook video advertising is not as easy, fast or simple as the normal ads, since you need to create a video. However, it will be well worth your time because the results will be so much more impactful. The following are some common mistakes I recommend you to avoid:

- **Not embracing mobile video marketing:** A large part of your videos will be viewed on a mobile device. Make sure you take this into account while creating the video. It's a good practice to watch your video on a mobile phone or tablet before uploading it to Facebook and make sure it offers a nice viewing experience. Most Facebook users visit the site via Facebook mobile application, so being able to create relevant videos for the mobile audience will help to obtain good results.

- **Not taking enough time and effort to create your video:** Don't just use any video, but rather, carefully follow the guidelines outlined in this Chapter. It will take some time at first, but the results you can generate with a good video outweigh the time you will spend on the creation process. Facebook users see the video ad on their own News Feed on Facebook, so the video better be relevant and interesting for them, or else it will be ignored.

- **Making the video too long and boring:** Focus on creating short videos that are fast moving, communicating the message clearly, and having a clear call to action indicating what users can do next if they want to know more.

- **Not creating a good introduction for your video:** The first 2-4 seconds of your video are the most crucial and it's during those first seconds that the viewer will decide if he or she will continue watching the video. Creating a lot of movement or using different colors during the first seconds is a recommended practice. Watch other video ads on Facebook, and take notes on what techniques they use to get people's attention during the first 3 seconds.

- **Not using an attractive thumbnail image:** Facebook allows you to upload a thumbnail image for each video. If you fail to do this, a random image will be selected for you, typically making the impact far less powerful than if you create a specific thumbnail image for each video. Canva.com is the recommended tool, as I have mentioned several times before in this book.

In the example below, you can see the thumbnail image used by the Pillsbury company for one of its recipe videos, which is very relevant for people interesting in preparing food.

Figure 7.1: Example video ad from Pillsbury.

- Not analyzing the results: Don't just create a video and check how many views it got. Make the effort to learn the most crucial video advertising metrics presented later in this Chapter of the book.

- Not recognizing that sometimes video ads are on mute: Users need to tap into the video to turn on the sound. Therefore you can use a small text reminding them to turn on the audio. You can also try to create video ads which communicate their message even if they are muted, since some viewers don't turn on the audio.

63. Use videos to get more repeat customers

Facebook remarketing and Lookalike Audiences, combined with video marketing, is a powerful mix that can quickly increase the return on investment of your campaigns. As mentioned earlier in this book, Facebook remarketing allows you to show ads to people who are on your email list or customer list, or have visited certain pages of your website.

All small businesses should start using video ads targeting their current clients or website visitors, as they will allow you to show them testimonials from your previous customers or quick videos answering questions other customers have asked.

Currently, this type of video ad is probably the most effective and brings the most return on investment, as the audience is someone who already knows your company, but just needs a bit more information before buying your product.

64. Types of videos you can use

In Chapter four of this book, I listed four types of videos your company should create and upload to your Facebook Page:

- Short video tutorials.
- Video testimonials and case-study videos.
- Slideshow videos or templated videos.

- Video presentations of products, the company, or employees.

You can read specific descriptions of each of these video types in Chapter four.

Probably the quickest and easiest type of video ads to create are slideshow videos or templated videos produced by an online tool such as Veeroll.com, which I will cover later in this Chapter. Each company should test different videos like these to see what works best for them.

Sharing valuable tips and information with the people who view your video can be surprisingly beneficial. One of my clients created a three-minute video promoting their paid training event. During the first 20 seconds of the video they did not mention anything about their promotion, but shared a valuable tip. To their surprise, a large number of people who saw that video also shared it on Facebook because it was perceived as a valuable video rather than as an advertising video. This is a proper example of the effectiveness of videos which don't seems like typical video ads, but rather share useful information with the viewer. Try creating these types of videos and making them interesting and relevant to your ideal clients.

65. Get impressive results by using the correct audience targeting

Before creating your video, take time to consider how to find the most relevant audience on Facebook. You can review the Facebook targeting options in the Facebook Advertising Strategies Chapter of this book.

Once you have clarity on your target audience, make sure the following elements are relevant to your target audience:

- Images in your video ad.
- Content of your video ad.
- Video thumbnail for your video ad.
- Call to action in your video ad.

All of those four elements should be in synch and very interesting to your target audience.

Here is a screenshot of the results for one of my clients who runs a dog training company in Mallorca, Spain and has gained excellent results from Facebook video ads by making them extremely relevant for the target audience.

Results that this campaign produced were:

- Video views: 3,314.
- Amount spent: 7.33 Euros (approximately 8 USD).
- Cost per video view: 0.002 Euros (approximately 0.0021 USD).

Figure 7.2: Results of the video advertising campaign.

It's worth noting that Facebook counts a video view when someone watches the first 3 seconds of the video. Therefore, not all of these 3,314 viewers watched the video until the end. Nevertheless, they are still quite impressive results. If you pay only 0.002 euros per video view, you can generate 50,000 video views with 100 euros (approximately 109 USD).

These kinds of results are possible when the target audience is carefully defined and the video offers a lot of movement and interesting content in the first few seconds. If the video is not relevant for the target audience and they are not engaging with the video, your Facebook video will end up being a waste of money.

66. Create powerful video ads with Veeroll

Veeroll is the most powerful video advertising tool that offers ready-made templates you can use for video ads. Using Veeroll saves you a lot of time and enables you to create compelling videos within few seconds.

This online tool is quite easy to use and something that should be tested out by all companies interested in getting better at video advertising. When using Veeroll you can select the type of template that fits best for your campaign and then personalize it with text and information. A few minutes after creating your video, Veeroll will give you a link to download the video you just created, which you can then upload to Facebook.

Additionally, Veeroll provides extensive training and is constantly working on new Facebook video ad templates.

Figure 7.3: Some of the templates Veeroll offers for creating Facebook video ads.

EXPERT OPINION – Gideon Shalwick

"One of the biggest opportunities online right now is running video ads on social media sites like Facebook, YouTube, Twitter and Instagram.

Because there is a 'perceived' barrier to entry with video ads, competition is still very low compared to traditional paid advertising options. Which means... You can get extremely targeted, highly engaged traffic to your site at very low costs. Which competent entrepreneur would not want that for their own business?

All you need to get started is a compelling but short video that extols all the wonderful features of your wizzbang new product or service, pop it onto the right platform (for example Facebook video ads or YouTube video ads), and you're on your way to a whole new world of excellent traffic sources.

A simple way to make sure that your video ad converts into views, leads and sales is to use a powerful sales formula for creating your videos. We often use the formula AIDCA:"

*A stands for **Attention**.*
*I for **Interest/Intrigue**.*
*D for **Desire**.*
*C for **Conviction**.*
*A for **Action**.*

"This formula helps us to craft highly effective video ad scripts. And then we simply use existing templates to automatically create these videos for us - no need for fancy gear or expensive video production teams!

So far, we've been getting STELLAR results from these very simple templated video ads. Recently we ran a simple split test to see how well a professionally produced 'talking head' video would compare against one of the templated videos we use. The results presented in the image below were nothing short of amazing.

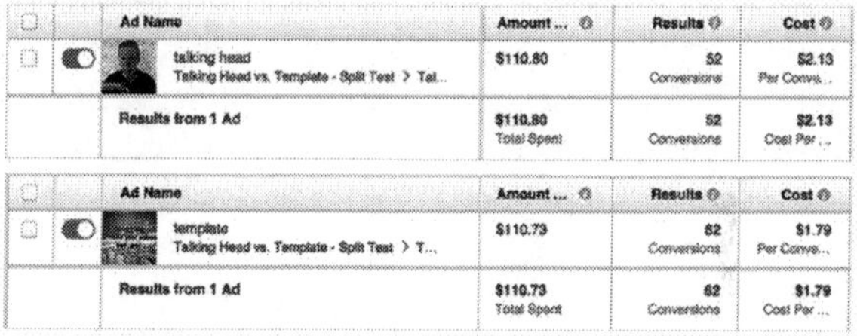

Ad Name	Amount ...	Results	Cost
talking head Talking Head vs. Template - Split Test > Tal...	$110.80	52 Conversions	$2.13 Per Conve...
Results from 1 Ad	$110.80 Total Spent	52 Conversions	$2.13 Cost Per ...

Ad Name	Amount ...	Results	Cost
template Talking Head vs. Template - Split Test > T...	$110.73	62 Conversions	$1.79 Per Conve...
Results from 1 Ad	$110.73 Total Spent	62 Conversions	$1.79 Cost Per ...

Figure 7.4: Results from the video advertising campaign by Gideon Shalwick.

FAs you can see in the image above, the templated video ad OUTPERFORMED the professional talking head video - which is quite a feat in and of itself when you consider how little effort went into creating the templated video ad!

The templated video ad sent us new leads for a mere $1.79 per lead, whereas the fancy talking head video cost us $2.13!"

"While video advertising is already a very lucrative opportunity not to be missed, I strongly believe that we are only at the beginning of a massive new trend right now. Which means, if you're serious about driving tons of the right kind of traffic to your site, now is one of the best times to jump on the video advertising train!"

Gideon Shalwick
Co-Founder,
Veeroll.com

67. Test different mobile apps to create your video

There are a wide range of different mobile applications that allow you to create quick and short videos. Most of these apps work for creating slideshow videos or short videos that are comprised of photos and video clips. Probably the most well known app is Magisto, which is free and available on iOS and Android operating systems. There are a lot of other apps, but you might want to start with Magisto.

Figure 7.5: Magisto application.

These types of slideshow videos help to share your product offerings or information about certain new product launches. When creating a video, remember to keep it fast moving and optimized for mobile viewing, as mentioned earlier in this Chapter.

Not all of your videos should be slideshow videos, as your ideal clients also want to see the faces of your employees and might get bored if you only promote slideshow videos.

Link to download Magisto for iPhone:
https://itunes.apple.com/us/app/magisto-video-editor-movie/id486781045

Link to download Magisto for Android:
https://play.google.com/store/apps/details?id=com.magisto&hl=en

Facebook has its own slideshow video creation tool, but it's currently still quite rudimentary, and I recommend using other more professional tools and applications.

68. Upload and optimize your video on Facebook

Here are the quick steps for creating your first video ad. This is a simple walk-through showing the main options, but not all the small details. Remember that Facebook ad creation interphase changes periodically, so it might look a bit different than in this example.

- **Select your ad objective:** As will all Facebook advertising, the ad creation process starts at *www.facebook.com/ads/create*. First you select the ad objective. Video ads can be used with the following advertising objectives:

- Boost your posts.

- Promote your page.

- Send people to your website.

- Increase conversions on your website.

- Get installs of your app.

- Increase engagement in your app.

- Get video views.

- Select the target audience: After selecting your ad objective, on the next page you select the target audience for your video ad (follow the guidelines shared earlier in the book).

- Select budget and bidding options: Choose how much you want to spend. Start with a small daily amount, testing your results, so you can increase the amount when you start getting good results, or pause the campaign if the video ad does not work.

Typically it's good to start with automatic bidding, which helps you to get the greatest amount of views at the best price.

Figure 7.6: Facebook video ad budget and bidding options.

- Upload your video: on the next page you can upload your video to Facebook. As shown in the picture above, the following are the specifications for video ads.

- Format: .MOV or .MP4 files.
- Resolution: at least 720p.
- Recommended aspect ratio: widescreen (16:9).
- Facebook: 60 minutes max. (2.3 GB).

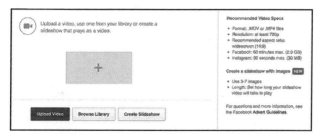

Figure 7.7: Video uploading process.

- Select video thumbnail: After uploading your video, Facebook prompts you to upload a video thumbnail or choose from different images taken from the video.

- Select text, links and location of your video ad:

- **Text:** Try to start the text with a question, which normally generates more engagement and gets viewers' attention.

- **Call to action:** choose the most relevant call to action from the following options: shop now, book now, learn more, signup, download, and watch more.

- **Website URL:** Enter the URL you want to direct viewers to after watching the video.

- **Choose where you want your video ad to be shown:** Normally video ads work best on desktop

News Feeds and mobile News Feeds. I tend to remove the option of showing the video ad on the right hand column, as it is a less effective alternative.

Figure 7.8: Screenshot of Facebook ad creation process where you select text, URL and location of the ad.

Finally, you can click on "Review Order," which enables you to review a summary of the new video campaign you have created, or "Place Order" to start your campaign.

Facebook Power Editor can also be used for the video ad creation process. It offers some additional options like the possibility to use longer text with your video and the opportunity to create a lot of similar campaigns quickly.

69. Gain valuable insights by analyzing video advertising metrics

Probably the most important part of a successful video ad campaign is the analysis of the results. First define the most essential metrics of your campaign. They might be the amount of revenue generated or the number of new email signups. Those are the numbers you want to carefully track in each video campaign, to learn which ads work most effectively.

In addition, you should track other key metrics related to your video ad. At Facebook Ad Manager (*www.facebook.com/ads/manager*), you can find 11 different metrics (image below) related to the performance of your video ad. For example, it is useful to know what percentage of the viewers saw 25% and how many saw 50% of the video.

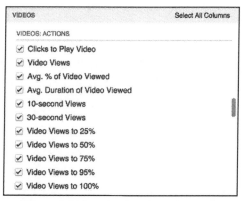

Figure 7.9: Facebook video ad metrics.

Video Retention Data helps you to learn how you can improve your videos. In the example presented in the image below, you can see an audience retention graph from a video with a boring and ineffective start. As you can observe, during the first 12 seconds the video loses viewers, but after the 12-second mark the viewers start to pay more attention and continue watching the content.

This type of information is vital to improve and to make more effective videos.

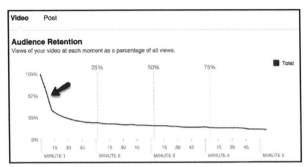

Figure 7.10: Audience Video Retention Graph can be found on Facebook Page insights and it is shown for the videos you upload to your Facebook page.

70. Learn from frequently asked questions about Facebook video ads

The following are some common questions I receive from people who are starting with Facebook video ads.

Can I create Facebook video ads while running other Facebook ads?

Sure, you can run as many ads simultaneously as needed, just remember to visit Facebook Ads Manager at www.facebook.com/ads/manager on a daily basis to review the ad performance.

What types of videos ads are the most valuable for my business?

It depends on the type of business you operate, but normally all businesses should use video testimonials and customer stories, as they serve to increase credibility toward your company.

I would also recommend creating several videos showcasing your products and employees, and also trying some short slideshow videos.

Showing the faces of people who work for your company is an important credibility booster and helps your company to be perceived as more "human."

Can I use the videos I have on YouTube as Facebook video ads?

You can do it, but I would edit and improve them before uploading them to Facebook. Typically, a YouTube video is a bit more slow-paced and doesn't have an interesting enough beginning to catch people's interest, as is necessary for a Facebook video ad. Some of my clients have gained great results by editing YouTube videos and optimizing them for the Facebook environment.

EXPERT OPINION – Kevin Davis

"In this case study you will see the results we got for a client of mine based in Australia who sells fishing lessons. This was a very successful campaign where we used Facebook video advertising combined with a Facebook contest.

In the images below, you can see the video ad we used for the Barra Basics fishing course, which had the following results:

Leads directly from ad: 1948
Leads through referrals: 320
Total leads through campaign: 2,268

This campaign was focused on an audience that liked fishing related interests in Queensland and Northern Territory in Australia, where most Barramundi fishing is done in Australia."

Figure 7.11: Example Facebook News Feed advertisement.

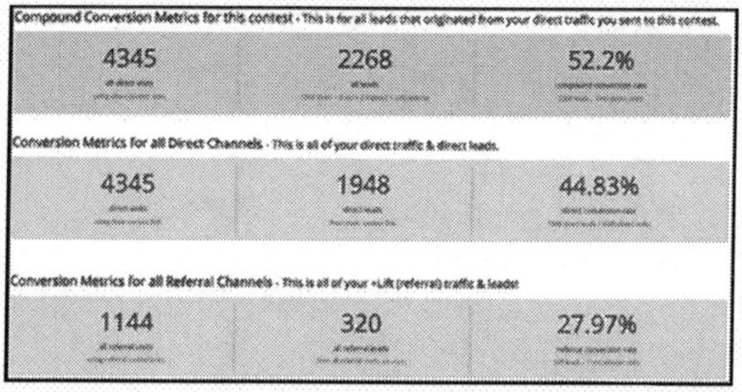

Figure 7.12: Results from Contest Domination

"When creating your video ad, there are three key ingredients to keep in mind to get the best results.

1) Make sure your video is moving and engaging. In this case, it highlighted the expert and his client catching trophy fish.

2) Keep the video short and include a clear call to action message in the final third of the video.

3) Be sure to include a clear call to action in the description as well and include a link to your landing page in the description so that even if they don't watch the whole video, they can still click over to your landing page.

We have seen video ads work best with a giveaway or contest type of an offer. To manage our contest offers we use Contest Domination, which handles all of the requirements for running a contest on Facebook."

Kevin Davis
Paid Traffic Strategist
www.paidtraffic.co

THREE SUGGESTED ACTION STEPS FROM CHAPTER 7:

Here are three suggested action steps related to the content of this Chapter. Try to complete these before moving to the next Chapter.

- Before starting with Facebook video advertising, study the common mistakes other advertisers make shared in strategy 62 and get ready to avoid them.

- Create a list of what your first three video ads could be about. Create your first video ad campaign following the step by step instructions in strategy 68.

- Carefully study the frequently asked questions (strategy 70), as those will help you to attain better results.

CHAPTER 8

Instagram Marketing Strategies

Instagram was the first major social network that is a mobile app only, meaning that you cannot create an account for it or post content on it from a desktop computer. Facebook bought Instagram for $1 billion in 2012 and today it is one of the most important social networks in many sectors. With over 400 million active users and growing, Instagram is a more relevant and important social network for small business than other social networks like Twitter and Pinterest.

Some of the industries in which businesses are having a lot of success with Instagram are fashion, tourism, fitness, food, home and living, and the auto industry. But all kinds of companies can benefit from marketing with Instagram when conducted correctly, and I encourage you to start testing these strategies.

In this Chapter you will discover creative Instagram strategies and in the next one how to use Instagram advertising.

Figure 8.1: Instagram main website at www.instagram.com.

71. Learn basic Instagram strategies before you start sharing content

Here are some basic strategies you need to know before starting to post content.

- **Do a quick search on how other companies in your sector use Instagram:** You can search on Google your competitor's Instagram profiles. This search can be done on a desktop computer even if you don't have an Instagram account.

    You may also consider visiting the Instagram profiles of some big brands just to get the feel of how they use this medium.

    Here are some well-known brands that conduct successful Instagram marketing:
    www.instagram.com/nike
    www.instagram.com/starbucks
    www.instagram.com/lego
    www.instagram.com/xbox

    To find more of these, simply use the same URL structure as in the earlier examples and replace the brand name with the name of the company you want to search.

- **Take time to edit the photos or videos you post:** You want to share quality content and generate a positive user experience for the Instagram users who view your content. Later in this Chapter you will discover several apps which can be used to help you to edit the photos and videos to make them more impactful.

- **Try to post a lot of content:** Some small businesses simply open their Instagram accounts, post few photos and then forget about their account. Try to be active by responding to comments and questions and posting a lot of interesting content. To get the maximum benefit, it is recommended to share 1 – 3 photos or videos every day.

- **Be creative and different:** Avoid posting boring images of your company logo or product catalogue. Instead, show your employees in their environment and share images from places your clients don't have access to. For example, a restaurant could share a short video showing how they cook one delicious dish in the kitchen.

72. Set up your Instagram profile correctly

Instagram can be a great tool for small businesses. If you want to experience the full range of benefits that this social media network can offer for your company, it is important to set up your profile correctly from the start.

Take the following steps to maximize your success on Instagram:

- **Download the app:** Unlike some other social media tools that allow you to create accounts through a desktop browser, Instagram profiles can only be created through their apps, which are available for Android and iOS users.

- **Become familiar with this social network:** To gain insight into the ways that Instagram can be used to boost a business, take some time to visit the profiles of at least 10 companies in your industry. See what they are doing well and what they could be doing better in order to benefit from their experience. Also take some time to look up some of the biggest brands that are currently using Instagram as a business tool, companies like Starbucks, Apple Music, and American Eagle.

- **Create an account name:** When possible, this should be your company name. If that name is already taken, keep it as similar to your brand or business name as possible, allowing customers to find you quickly and easily.

- **Add a profile picture:** As you looked at the other companies that are successfully using Instagram to connect with their audiences, you may have noticed that the profile pictures are not always a simple logo. It's important to ensure that your picture not only represents your business well, but also connects with your audience. Consumers want to know that there is a human presence behind the business, and not feel like they are just interacting with a corporation.

- **Write a short bio:** Keep your description short and professional, but also add a touch of personality. Don't forget to provide a link to your landing page and basic contact information, when possible.

- **Optimize your settings:** Make sure that you don't exclude potential followers by setting your account to "private."

As you begin to use Instagram for your business, remember to provide links to and from your other social media sites so that customers can get to all of your content quickly and easily. By also including links in your email signature and on your business cards, you can leverage and multiply the effect that your content has on your customers, giving them opportunities to engage with your brand in meaningful ways on a regular basis.

73. Avoid common Instagram mistakes

Typical mistakes most small businesses commit when starting to use Instagram for the first time are as follows:

- **Not being active:** Don't just create your account and wait, assuming that everyone will find you and follow you. Start posting content, following interesting people and companies, and engaging with other Instagram users.

- **Not responding to comments quickly:** As a company you need to monitor your Instagram activity and respond in a timely manner to any questions or comments. The person who is responsible for managing Instagram for your company should have notifications set up in his or her mobile phone that alert him or her every time there is a new comment on Instagram.

- **Posting the same type of content all the time:** Be creative and test different types of photos. You want to surprise your followers every now and then with new and creative content. Also use the tips related to video content shared later in this Chapter.

- **Not following new people:** Constantly follow new influential people in your sector and also your clients so that you can engage with them.

- **Not editing your photos:** Before uploading to Instagram, try to edit your photos. You can use Canva.com (on a desktop) or a mobile application like Over (available on iOS and Android). These editing apps allow you to add text or artwork on top of your images, making them more attractive looking.

74. Use the correct hashtag strategy

Hashtags, also called as tags, are a vital part of Instagram. They allow you to describe your photos and relate them back to your business while also helping to direct followers to new content. For every post you make on Instagram, you should include roughly 8-11 hashtags that are relevant to your business, maximizing the benefits of hashtags without inserting too many.

Here are some tips for finding hashtags:

- **Determine the best hashtags that relate to your product:** Select the magnifying glass icon at the bottom of the app and type in a keyword. If you own a travel agency, you may simply type "travel" into the search bar at the top. Instagram will then show you all of the top related hashtags. This can help you to determine which keywords users are searching for and posting about.

Figure 8.2: Example of how to find most popular hashtags on Instagram.

- **Review your competition:** See what hashtags others in your business sector are using and take a look at how customers are responding to them.

- **Create your own unique tags:** This is a great way to build customer involvement with your brand. Say that you are sponsoring a 5K fundraiser and own a coffee shop. You might come up with something like #5KCoffeeDash and promote it at your physical business, encouraging followers to post their own pictures using the tag on their own Instagram accounts.

- **Use local hashtags:** Incorporate your city into your hashtags to increase the likelihood that tourists and locals are able to associate your business with your location.

- **Check out top hashtags that are currently trending worldwide:** You can find these top hashtags at *http://websta.me/hot.* Remember that many of these are not business related, so only use ones that are actually relevant to your business.

Once you have decided on hashtags that you'd like to use repeatedly, save them to your phone for quick access. You can also visit Instagram photos you have posted earlier and add new hashtags into comments for additional promotion.

75. Improve your content by using these three Instagram applications

If you're looking to make your Instagram content more compelling and interesting for your customers, and encourage them to engage with your brand, there are several great tools you can use. Each one of these tools is free, easy to use, and made by Instagram, which means that they are well supported and updated regularly.

CREATE ANIMATED GIFs USING THE BOOMERANG APPLICATION

When you want to add a little bit of life to your Instagram content, you can use Boomerang to create an animated GIF. An animated GIF (Graphics Interchange Format) is basically a short set of images with looped movement. This is a great strategy to help your content catch the eyes of your followers. Boomerang is also great for business owners who want their content to make an emotional connection with their followers, making them laugh or making them think through a short, focused loop.

Figure 8.3: Boomerang application.

USE HYPERLAPSE TO MAKE FAST-MOVING VIDEOS

Consumers today have short attention spans. With the double and triple speed settings available through Hyperlapse, you can share meaningful videos without making your followers engage for long periods of time. There are a number of ways that you can use this kind of video to share information with your clients. For example, if you want to provide an overview of an event that you've successfully completed or show your followers how to prepare a delicious dish from your restaurant, Hyperlapse can help you to do so effectively.

At this time, Hyperlapse is only available for iOS users, unlike the other tools that are mentioned here, which are available for both iOS and Android.

Figure 8.4: Hyperlapse application.

ENHANCE YOUR VISUAL STORYTELLING SKILLS WITH THE LAYOUT APP

The Layout app lets you seamlessly integrate several images into a single picture, allowing you to build a story. There are several ways to do this. For a boutique that sells vintage clothing, you may piece together several items, telling a story of how someone designed the perfect outfit for a night on the town.

Layout allows you to share multiple images in one place without flooding the feeds of your followers with a lot of individual pictures. By bringing together several pictures, you can catch the attention of your followers for a longer period of time and make it more likely for them to experience an emotional connection with your brand.

When you want your content to draw the interest of potential customers and encourage them to connect with your brand, these three tools are a great place to start.

Figure 8.5: Layout application.

76. Create a series of short videos on Instagram

Many small businesses fail to use one of the more powerful tools available on Instagram – short videos. Videos can add interest to your feed, share information with your followers, and give clients insight into the things that make your business unique. These videos don't have to be long – in fact, the recommended length is only 7-15 seconds.

Here are some top ideas for implementing video content on your Instagram feed:

- **Give your customers a glimpse of what happens behind the scenes:** Clients love to see personality in the businesses they follow. A great way to do this is to show a short compilation of your employees getting prepared for the day.

- **Demonstrate how your products are made:** People tend to value a product more when they realize how much craftsmanship goes into its design. Give a short overview of how your products came to be, allowing your customers to respond with questions.

- **Offer helpful tips:** This is an especially great idea for businesses that provide consultations or coaching, but can even be used for product-based businesses.

The more valuable content you share with your followers, the more they will start to like you and trust you.

- **Share comments from happy customers:** Put together several quick comments from satisfied customers sharing why they chose to patronize your business.

- **Display "before" and "after" pictures:** This is a great solution for weight loss companies, beauty salons, and other businesses that want to share visual results with their customers.

- **Show content at faster speeds:** Want to show something from beginning to end, but not make your customers sit for a long time to watch it? Use the double or triple speed options to share the same information in a fun way.

If you get stuck creatively, ask your best customers what kinds of video they would like to see and ask for their feedback on your content. With a little bit of time and practice, you can enjoy the benefits that short videos on Instagram can offer for business owners.

77. Draw user attention with video collages using PicPlayPost

There are a number of helpful applications for improving your content on Instagram, but definitely my favorite one is PicPlayPost, which only a few companies use. This app is available on iOS and Android, and allows you to create captivating videos and even GIF animations.

On Instagram, everything that is different and new will attract the user's attention. With PicPLayPost you can quickly and easily create video collages, showing several video clips that play simultaneously inside one video.

The image below shows an example of this type of video collage. It's a video for one restaurant showing three different dishes on a certain menu. This type of content surprises users, and makes them want to watch your content more carefully.

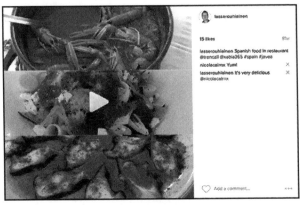

Figure 8.6: Example Instagram video created by PicPlayPost application.

Link to download PicPlayPost on iOS store
https://itunes.apple.com/us/app/picplaypost/id498127541

Link to download PicPlayPost on Google play store:
https://play.google.com/store/apps/details?id=com.flambe studios.picplaypost

78. Automate your Instagram content with Hootsuite

When you run a small business and are looking to attract and engage potential customers through social media channels, it can be difficult to find the time to do everything that you need to do in order to be successful. Hootsuite is a particularly powerful automation tool that can offer unique benefits for business owners who utilize Instagram.

Hootsuite is a product designed to make social media account management easier and more effective for business owners. It integrates over eight different social media networks into one place, allowing users to pre-schedule posts, engage directly with customers, and see all of their social media content within a single application.

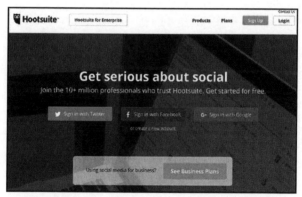

Figure 8.7: Home page of Hootsuite.com.

ADVANTAGES OF HOOTSUITE FOR INSTAGRAM MANAGEMENT

There are numerous benefits for businesses that use Hootsuite to manage their Instagram accounts. Hootsuite offers flexible scheduling so that your content can be automatically posted at preset times, ensuring that your pictures reach your followers at times that are convenient to them and maximizing the impact of each post. Additionally, Hootsuite allows you to engage with your clients, track your competitors, and observe best practices for businesses like yours. Their analytics tools can also help you to see if your social media strategies are currently working well or if they may need to be adapted along the way.

As a business owner, your time is valuable. It's important that social media management doesn't eat into the time that you need to be able to focus on the tasks that only you can do within your company. Hootsuite makes it easy to delegate Instagram tasks to other members of your organization, while giving you oversight of their activities along the way. If you invest in a number of social media technologies, Hootsuite can also manage many of these tools in one place, saving time and energy for you and your team.

No technology is perfect. Posts scheduled for Instagram through Hootsuite require some steps to be taken manually, which means that the process is not fully automated. Additionally, there may be a learning curve to the interface and reporting features available in the Hootsuite app.

79. Use emojis correctly on Instagram

Emojis, which are also known as emoticons, are small images that help to communicate emotions. They are often used in social media forms such as Facebook and Skype, as well as instant messaging services, text messages, and emails. While they may seem small and silly, they can actually be very powerful when used correctly on Instagram. In the context of Instagram, emojis are best used in the descriptions of photos and in comments.

Figure 8.8: Different emojis you can use on Instagram.

Studies have shown that businesses have great results when they use emojis to add a sense of emotion or feeling to written text. Because users have positive associations with emojis, using them in your content can help you to build trust with your clients, making it easy for them to decide to purchase through your company. These little characters can help to show the human side of your business.

Emojis should be used with consideration and intentionality. If you haven't used them on Instagram before, take a look through business and personal posts to see how they can be used well. When using emojis, consider what they will communicate and don't overuse them within your content. However, by sprinkling them into your communication through Instagram, you can increase the positive interactions you have with your followers.

80. Learn from frequently asked questions about Instagram

Is it recommended to use user-generated content?

Yes, encourage your clients and customers to share photos of your business and products on Instagram using a certain hashtag. You can use the application called "Repost for Instagram" to share these photos on your Instagram, giving credit to the authors of the content.

Typically, the user-generated content is more interesting and relevant to your clients than content created by your company.

What are some tools I can use to see analytics of my Instagram account?

For a long time the most well-known Instagram analytics application was IconoSquare, but it recently removed the "free" option, and is now a paid tool. Other similar applications that can give you insights into your Instagram activity are socialinsight.io, *www.crowdfireapp.com* and *https://minter.io*.

In addition, Simply Measured offers a free Instagram analytics report of your account at *http://simplymeasured.com/freebies/instagram-analytics*.

Use these tools to get clarity as to what type of content works best for you, and to generate more of it.

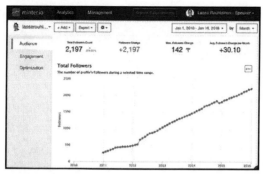

Figure 8.9: Analysis of my Instagram account by Minter.io.

Should all my posts be about my company and its products?

No, that would be boring for your followers. Think from the point of view of your audience and what could be interesting content for them. For example, local events or happenings or photos related to certain times of the year like Christmas, etc...

Also, don't use calls to action in all of your photos, but rather build trust and credibility by sharing interesting advice and photos that have nothing to do with your business.

THREE SUGGESTED ACTION STEPS FROM CHAPTER 8:

Here are three suggested action steps related to the content of this Chapter. Try to complete these before moving to the next Chapter.

- If you are not currently on Instagram, set up your profile following the recommendations in strategy 72. If you already have an account, make sure you have configured your account according to these tips.

- Download the three suggested applications for Instagram marketing according to strategy 75. Also download PicPlayPost as recommended in strategy 77.

- Learn from the most frequently asked questions (strategy 80), as they offer other valuable ideas you can implement in your Instagram marketing.

CHAPTER 9

Instagram Advertising Strategies

In 2015 Instagram opened its advertising platform to everyone, and currently Instagram ads offers a great opportunity, as the platform does not have as much competition as Facebook ads does.

Before reading this Chapter, I recommend that you review all the tips and strategies covered earlier in this book regarding Facebook advertising strategies, as there are many similarities between the two.

81. Understand the Basic Instagram ad formats

Right now, Instagram offers three different kinds of ads, although there is the possibility that more will be added to their services in the future. Unlike the ads that can be created for Facebook, Instagram ads are only able to be viewed on mobile devices. So, as you design your ads for Instagram, keep in mind the ways that your content should be optimized for mobile viewing.

The three ad formats available through Instagram are as follows:

- **Photo ads:** These use a single static image to present a product or offer. When using photo ads, make sure that your image is relevant to your business. Check out the ads for other businesses in your sector to see what works best for your target audience.

- **Video ads:** These are similar to Facebook video ads, so review that Chapter for best practices. Remember to use movement and color to keep your content interesting and give a clear call to action to maximize your impact. Instagram now supports videos up to a minute long, which can be viewed in portrait or landscape mode.

- **Carousel ads:** These ads consist of a series of related images. They are particularly helpful for companies that showcase a lot of products, such as fashion or e-commerce companies, and can be a great way to tell a story through your ad.

Most advertisers begin their campaigns with photo ads, but you can test out the various kinds of ads available through Instagram to see which will work best for you.

Before creating your own ads, take screenshots of the ads you see on Instagram and analyze what was good about them or how they could be improved. All Instagram ads have the word sponsored in the top right hand corner of the ad and a call to action button below the ad.

82. Learn to master the three essential elements of Instagram Ads

Figure 9.1: Example Instagram ad.

There are three different components that make up each successful Instagram ad:

- **Creative (photo or video):** This is the most important component of your ad. Take time planning and creating creative elements that could catch the interest of your ideal clients. The ideal size of the image is 1080 x 1080 pixels. If you use a video in your ad, the size should not be bigger than 30 MB. Videos are muted on Instagram, and the user needs to tap into the video in order to turn on the sound.

- **Call to action button:** Each Instagram ad will come up with a call to action button that appears just under the ad image. At the time of writing this book, Facebook allows you to use eight different calls to action on Instagram ads. The possible calls to action can be seen in the image below.

Figure 9.2: Different calls to action you can use with Instagram Ads.

- **Caption text:** Try to start with a question. Focus on the end result your ideal client will get when clicking on your ad. Currently the character limit is 300 characters and it is not recommended to use a website link, as it cannot be a clickable link.

83. Create an Instagram account

If you don't already have an Instagram account, I recommend creating one according to the guidelines described in the previous Chapter. Follow other companies and accounts in your sector and try to get a feel for how they use Instagram. Also analyze how they respond to comments and engage with their followers.

There is a way to create Instagram ads without having an Instagram account; all you would need is a Facebook Business Page. However, this is not a recommended practice as it has the following drawbacks:

- **You cannot respond to comments people write on your ad.** This is a big disadvantage, as engagement is an important part of the Instagram ads.
- **Your Facebook page and image will be used on your ad.** When people click on it, they will not be taken to your Instagram profile (since you don't have one) and that might confuse people and generate distrust, as some people want to visit the Instagram profile of the advertiser to learn more about them.

84. Respect and follow Instagram ad quality guidelines

As you design Instagram ads, it is important to follow the ad quality guidelines. Set aside time to plan ways to make your ads relevant to your target audience. The best ads are useful to potential clients. Ads should avoid sounding like spam or promising something that's too good to be true.

These practices are not only unprofessional, but can hurt your brand instead of help it.

The best way to create a positive ad experience for your customer is to keep your text, images, and landing page (the web page your ad will lead to) relevant to each other and to your product or service.

Instagram has several guidelines to help you to know what to avoid in an ad. Note that having too many ads rejected may cause your account to be flagged or suspended by Instagram.

Here are some common things to avoid:

- Bad image quality (including unclear images or strange cropping).
- Unclear writing (including grammar and punctuation errors).
- Irrelevant links, images, or descriptions.

Just as you should for Facebook ads, you should read and review the Instagram ad policies at *www.facebook.com/policies/ads.*

85. Start your first Instagram advertising campaign

Starting to run your ads on Instagram is quite a similar process to that of running Facebook ads. Here are the basic steps you need to take in order to create your first ad:

- On Facebook Business Manager (which can be found at *business.facebook.com*), connect your Instagram account with your Facebook ad account.

- Go to _www.facebook.com/ads/create_ and select an objective for your Instagram ad. The most common ad objectives used for Instagram ads are "Clicks to Website" and "Video Views."

- Select the target audience, scheduling, and a budget for your ad, as you would do when creating a Facebook ad campaign. Notice that an estimate will be given on what is your potential daily reach on Instagram, as shown in the image below.

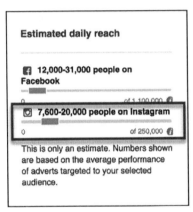

Figure 9.3: Example of an estimated daily reach on Instagram.

This estimate is calculated according to your target audience and your daily budget.

Upload the content of your ad, which can be an image or a video. The image you use on Instagram needs to be at least 600 × 315 pixels (you can always change the image size using _www.canva.com_). Ideally your image would be a square (1:1). After uploading your image, you can click on the small crop icon on the button in the right hand corner of the image.

This will open a tool that allows you to easily crop your image so that the version shown on Instagram is a square.

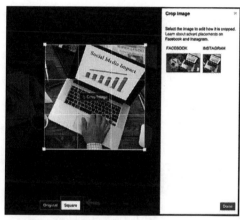

Figure 9.4: Facebook cropping tool allows you to crop your image so it's a square.

- **Connect your Instagram account:** When you create your Instagram ad for the first time, you need to connect your Instagram account. Click on the button that has the text "Add an Account." A pop-up window will open where you can enter the username and password of your account to connect your Instagram account.

Figure 9.5: Connect Instagram account for advertising.

- **Select what text and call to action you want to use:** Enter the text you want to use with your ad, keeping in mind that the limit is 300 characters, and choose a call to action button that will be shown under your ad image (see the image below as an example).

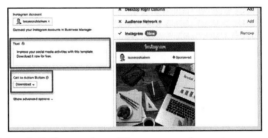

Figure 9.6: Screenshot of Instagram ad creation process.

- **Select the placement for your ad:** Naturally your ad will be shown on Instagram, but additionally you can choose if you want to advertise it also on Facebook Mobile News Feed.

- To start your campaign click on **Place Order** button.

The Instagram ad creation process can also be done in Facebook Power Editor, but here I covered how it is done in Facebook Ads Manager, as most users will use that option.

86. Test Facebook and Instagram ads together

One great way to maximize your social media campaigns without spending a lot of extra time and money is to use the Facebook ad platform to create both Facebook and Instagram ads. Because you are only dealing with one interface, it's fairly simple to learn how to do it, and therefore you'll spend less time creating your campaigns. As you create your ads, you can use the same targeting for audiences on both networks, defining the interests, demographics, and locations that you want to reach, and you will get to view the approximate number of people who will see your ads beforehand.

Reproducing the same campaign on both platforms has several benefits. Imagine that someone hops onto their Facebook page, sees your ad, and later, when they go to Instagram, they see the same ad. This can reinforce the original ad in their mind and make it feel like a much bigger campaign. This can be great for businesses, as it makes people feel like your company has an extensive reach. By testing your Facebook and Instagram ads together, you can multiply the effect of a single ad and experience better results.

After about 24 hours have passed, check on the analytics for your ad campaign and see if one platform is more effective than the other. If so, you can stop the secondary ad and continue with the more profitable one; otherwise, continue to use both.

87. Take into account Instagram ad image best practices

As I mentioned earlier, don't just use any random image in your ad, but rather carefully plan and create impactful ad images.

- **Be creative:** In the image below you can see a creative Instagram ad image which is different and catches users' attention.

Figure 9.7: Instagram ad image.

- **Test cartoon or graphic images:** In this other image below you can see an example of a cartoon image, which again is different than the usual images people see on Instagram.

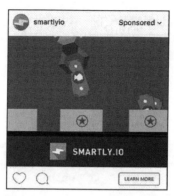

Figure 9.8: Instagram ad image.

- **Avoid using with too much white color:**
  Instagram's background color is white and therefore I
  recommend not using ads with a lot of white color in
  them since people who scroll quickly on their
  Instagram feeds probably won't notice these kind of
  ads. In the image below you can see one ad image
  with a lot of white in it.

Figure 9.9: Instagram image ad example.

- **Test using an arrow directing attention to the call to action button:** On the bottom left corner of your ad image you can insert an arrow pointing the eye to the call to action button. An example of this practice can be seen in the image below. This can significantly increase the amount of clicks the ad receives.

Figure 9.10: Example of using an arrow to direct users' attention to calls to action.

In addition, keep in mind that you cannot use more than 20% of text in each ad image. This same rule applies to images used with Facebook advertising. You can use the following tool provided by Facebook to see if your image has less than 20% of text in it:
www.facebook.com/ads/tools/text_overlay.

88. Test as many images as possible on Instagram

Here is an expert opinion from Facebook and Instagram expert Rocco Baldassarre, who shares an interesting case study on how he helped one client to achieve great results by testing different images.

EXPERT OPINION – Rocco Baldassarre

"Old School Labs is a US based company whose mission is to create uncompromising, premium supplements for informed customers who demand the very best.

We decided to promote a product called Vintage Base (2-in-1- multivitamin with probiotics) using Instagram ads because we wanted to test if the fitness community on Instagram would generate a profitable cost per acquisition ratio (CPA). The goal of this campaign was to have CPA or cost for each sale of 10.

To compare the effectiveness of Instagram ads, we then decided to test our best audiences from desktop and mobile News Feeds on Facebook.

In the image below, you can see the results of the campaign over a 30-day period:"

- Total number of sales: 343.
- Cost for each sale: $5.60.
- Amount spent: $1,921.35.

Figure 8.11 Results of the Instagram campaign of Rocco Baldassarre

"When optimizing your Instagram campaigns, test as many images as possible. They influence the CPA (cost per acquisition) the most, and ad images lose effectiveness if they are shown too often to the same users."

Rocco Alberto Baldassarre
Founder and CEO
www.zebraadvertisement.com

89. Target your email list or website visitors on Instagram

Advertising to an audience that already knows you will always bring better results than advertising for people who are seeing your product or service for the first time. That is one of the main reasons why remarketing is a recommended practice.

In Chapter six of this book, we covered Facebook remarketing and how to create Facebook remarketing audiences including people who are on your email newsletter list or who have visited your website in the past. You can target these same audiences with Instagram ads. For example, you can target your email subscribers, reminding them about an ongoing promotion or offer you might have.

These types of campaigns tend to perform very well and generate cheaper cost per click and cost per sale ratios than typical interest-based ad targeting.

90. Learn from most frequently asked questions about Instagram Ads

How can I measure the results of my Instagram campaign?

It can be done in Facebook Ads Manager at *www.facebook.com/ads/manager*, the same place you analyze the results from your Facebook ad campaigns. In Facebook Ads Manager, you can also edit your Instagram ads.

With Twitter ads you can target a hashtag with your ad. Is that possible on Instagram?

Targeting a hashtags means that your ads would be shown when people search for a specific hashtag. At the time of writing this book, this option is not available, but Instagram might start to offer that option later.

Should I answer the comments people are writing on my Instagram ad?

Of course, the more comments and engagement you have for your ad, the better. It is recommended that you try to answer each comment or question in a timely manner.

How long can my video ads be on Instagram?

They should be between 3 and 30 seconds long.

THREE SUGGESTED ACTION STEPS FROM CHAPTER 9:

Here are three suggested action steps related to the content of this Chapter. Try to complete these before moving to the next Chapter.

- Take time to understand the basic Instagram ad format (strategy 81) and essential elements of Instagram Ads (strategy 82).
- Learn the basic Instagram ad guidelines shared in strategy 84.
- Review the Instagram ad image ideas shared in strategy 87 and make a list of your 3 first possible ads and what they might be about.

CHAPTER 10

Facebook Messenger and WhatsApp Strategies

Instant mobile messaging is quickly growing to become one of the most important forms of communication in the modern business world. Two Facebook-owned applications, WhatsApp and Facebook Messenger, are the most popular messaging apps offering innovative ways for companies to communicate with their customers.

Other similar apps include WeChat, Line and Skype, as well as Viber and Slack, which are mostly used for internal communication within companies. However, WhatsApp and Facebook Messenger are the most widely used, and in this Chapter you will discover a number of strategies in which these modern instant messaging apps can be used to help you to increase your sales.

In the beginning of this book I highlighted the importance of understanding your customer sales funnel. WhatsApp and Facebook Messenger serve as excellent tools to increase your sales conversions with people who already know your business or who are repeat buyers. Therefore, they are normally best for the people who are at the end of your sales funnel, who just want more information, and they should not be used as spam or to send unsolicited messages.

91. Gain trust by quickly responding to customer inquiries on Facebook

Would you like to gain an edge over your competitors? Responding quickly to customer comments and questions on Facebook can greatly help you to do that.

In today's world, consumers are extremely busy. They depend on their mobile devices to help them to send messages and they expect to receive a response quickly, especially when dealing with businesses. Much of this communication happens through Facebook Messenger.

Facebook now offers a message to consumers that showcase your company's response time to inquiries. These special messages can help you to increase the number of inquiries you receive, driving business to your site, because it encourages customers to "Message Now" and expect a fast response.

Figure 10.1: Text on Facebook Business Page indicating time company takes to answer customer inquiries.

Imagine that you want to buy an article of clothing, you have a question you want to ask and are comparing your options between two different sites: One site indicates that they respond to inquiries within an hour and the other does not have any indication of response time. You would probably be more likely to contact the business with the response time of within one hour.

Fast response time is increasingly important in modern business. If you have an excellent response time, Facebook will allow you, as the page administrator, to add a badge called "Very Responsive" to messages, which can offer extra validation that customers can rely on your service.

92. Recognize the huge impact Facebook Messenger will have on businesses

With over 800 million monthly active users, Facebook Messenger is one of the most popular apps in the world today. It was named as the fastest growing app in 2015, according to the Nielsen company.

Facebook is constantly developing Messenger and separating it out from the other components of Facebook. In particular, they are working to develop interesting applications for business through Facebook Messenger.

With Facebook Messenger, customers can contact a business through its Facebook Business Page, which can then start a conversation on Messenger. Many customers prefer this experience to the old way of having to search through a website to find the right email address to get in touch with the right person at a company, Now, they can search for the appropriate person right in the Messenger app and quickly message them.

Facebook has improved the experience on the business side by allowing companies to manage conversations and responses through the desktop interface, available at _www.messenger.com_. They have also included features that allow high-quality video calling to occur between users, which can be a helpful tool for businesses as well.

Figure 10.2: Facebook Messenger. Image credit Facebook at
www.messenger.com.

Facebook is currently working on several features that will enhance the ways that companies do business. In the future, you'll be able to do things like order a ride on Uber, book a hotel room, set up an itinerary for your trip, or make a payment, all through the Facebook Messenger app. They are also implementing a new digital assistant named "M" that will help users to find what they're looking for more quickly.

Facebook is also working hard to attract young customers to their service. Their main competitor for this audience is Snapchat, which is now improving their messaging functionality to compete with Facebook Messenger.

All of these features and trends will be vital to businesses as they develop their brands online and maximize the new tools available through Facebook.

93. Become familiar with the basic features of Facebook Messenger

Here is an overview of the basic things that you can currently do with Facebook Messenger for your business:

- **Send photos and videos to your clients:** If you are a real estate agent, you can send clients pictures of a home or a video tour and can even edit the images to draw attention to particular features. The editing tool is similar to the one in Snapchat, which is popular with the millennial generation. Always keep important videos and pictures readily available to be sent from your phone or computer, but remember to keep them short and to the point.

- **Send audio messages:** This can be a great tool for maintaining the "human" element of your business and can help you to communicate complex information quickly and efficiently. For example, if you own a gym and had a client asking about a particular package, a friendly audio message can offer more detail in less time than typing everything into text form.

- **Share business locations:** This feature is particularly helpful for travel-based industries that might want to share directions on how to get to their businesses.

- **Communicate with business associates through video calls:** This tool is wonderful as an alternative to Skype for those who do international business. Voice calls can be made for free over a Wi-Fi connection and are high quality.

- **Send animated GIFs:** When you want to communicate something visually, but in a quick manner, send an animated GIF. These have smaller file sizes than a video, but can be animated to showcase several images. This is a great option for restaurants or businesses that want to highlight their products.

- **Send money:** This feature is currently only available in the US. By using a credit card, you can send money to friends and colleagues. More access may be available for businesses in the future.

Figure 10.3: Sample Facebook Messenger message.

Stickers can also be sent through Facebook Messenger, but should not necessarily be used by every business, as stickers can be seen as a less professional communication tool. However, their usage is growing in popularity and you should become familiar with how they work.

94. Prepare for more advanced business applications coming soon through Businesses on Messenger

There are a number of features that Facebook is currently working on that will be launched soon to assist businesses. Right now, Facebook is testing a new application called Businesses on Messenger that will allow companies to effectively communicate with their clients both before and after they make a purchase. With over 50 million businesses currently using the Facebook Business Pages, this will provide an element of customer service that had previously been missing from the platform.

In its development of this tool, Facebook has partnered with Zendesk, one of the top cloud-based customer service tools on the market. Everline.com is one of the first to be allowed to beta-test this tool for full-service customer support. Customers will be able to receive notifications when their items arrive and ask questions of the customer support team along the way via Facebook Messenger. Facebook's goal will be to provide companies with the ability to offer seamless and frictionless customer service in a professional manner.

Some of the things you can look forward to are customized layouts that allow businesses to create order confirmations and standard communications.

To effectively prepare for this business tool, you can start to use Messenger from the web interface at *www.messenger.com* and prepare any vital information so that you can have it ready to send to customers at a moment's notice. Prepare your customer support team in advance so that they can respond quickly and effectively to inquiries and comments from your customers.

95. Get excited about the possibilities Facebook's new virtual assistant "M" will create

Facebook has been working on a new virtual assistant, known as "M." It will be similar in some ways to Apple's Siri or Google Now, but will also likely have features that are more powerful, allowing it to accomplish more complex tasks over time. Right now, M works on Facebook Messenger, but is only available for beta users.

At its launch, you will be able to ask M common questions, like *how the stock market is doing that day*, and receive a quick response with relevant links to further information.

However, more advanced features are also in the works. Imagine that you wanted to research your competitors in a specific sector. M could help you do so. If you wanted to open a law firm in London, you could use M to gather details about the three largest firms in the area. If you owned a restaurant and wanted to find out what your competitors' best dishes were, M could research online review sites and provide you with the answer. M will also be able to help you save time by performing tedious tasks like making a call to cancel services on your behalf.

In the beta release, M does not have access to other applications on your phone, like Siri does, but support for that feature may be added at a later date. While some of the initial features of M may be limited, it will be able to learn from your responses and improve over time, which is known as "deep learning." Business owners can expect to get things done more quickly and efficiently with this new tool.

96. Discover how WhatsApp offers big opportunities for business communication

With over 1 billion active users currently, WhatsApp has become a big player in the communication industry. Owned by Facebook, it is estimated that WhatsApps will reach 2-3 billion users in the next few years. With a large user base, companies are starting to take notice of the ways that consumers prefer to use WhatsApp for their communication.

Figure 10.4: WhatsApp's website at www.whatsapp.com.

Here are some of the benefits of using WhatsApp for your business:

- **It's free and easy to use:** With an intuitive interface, WhatsApp provides a great communication experience at no cost.

- **It offers fast response times:** Users are more likely to check their communication through this app than through their email or missed calls. In business, a huge time waster is waiting for calls to be returned. Because users can respond on-the-go, they are able to respond faster to messages sent through WhatsApp.

- **It replaces SMS messages (text messaging):** Although some industries, like major banks, may still use SMS, a number of businesses are turning to WhatsApp instead.

- **It offers an alternative to phone calls:** With free calls between users on Wi-Fi networks, WhatsApp can allow customers to call you if needed. While there are similar services, such as Skype, these other services are usually only used for placing calls between people who already know each other. This is not the case with WhatsApp.

- **It works with all mobile platforms:** Its wide reach is a big part of its explosive growth.

Companies are currently finding that consumers prefer to communicate through WhatsApp. With this interest from businesses, Facebook will soon launch WhatsApp for Business, offering a competitive edge for companies.

97. Take advantage of the benefits WhatsApp offers for businesses

During the last few years I have consulted with a wide range of companies on how they can leverage the growing popularity of WhatsApp. Almost all of them reported that they had surprisingly positive experiences when using WhatsApp with their clients and are excited to continue to utilize this new form of communication with their clients.

Here are some of the most common benefits for businesses using the app:

- **Speed:** WhatsApp is becoming the fastest way to send and receive information. Clients are more likely to see your content quickly and respond, making it a helpful tool, especially for repeat clients.

- **Opening ratio:** Users are more likely to open your messages than they are to open an email from your company.

- **Frequency of use:** Users are engaged with WhatsApp first thing in the morning, throughout the day, and before they go to bed at night.

- **Quality of communication:** Many users communicate with friends and family through WhatsApp. When you use it for business communication properly, you are more likely to be perceived with trust and loyalty.

- **Preferred by users:** Consumers enjoy the communication experience more than a traditional phone call.

- **Support for many kinds of messages:** WhatsApp allows companies to send voice and video messages, as well as text messages, which provides the opportunity to create more engaging content and build better relationships with potential customers.

- **Better conversion rates:** Businesses have found that potential customers are more likely to make a purchase when communication is done via WhatsApp than through email or over the phone.

- **Emoji support:** Companies that use WhatsApp can include emojis or emoticons to communicate emotions and build better relationships with clients.

Figure 10.5: Sample WhatsApp message.

Whenever you use WhatsApp, always avoid sending unsolicited messages (spam) to your clients, as it's highly likely that the recipients will identify that message as spam and block you. If several users mark your number as blocked, WhatsApp might eliminate your user account.

Another common mistake to avoid is adding clients who don't know each other to a WhatsApp group. This is not a recommended practice and will only annoy the users.

98. Use a separate number for your WhatsApp and promote it

In some cases, business owners have shared their personal phone numbers with clients and quickly become overwhelmed by the number of WhatsApp messages they had to deal with on their personal devices.

To address this issue, it is important to get a separate phone number that is only used for company communication and especially for WhatsApp. It is fairly inexpensive to add a phone number for most businesses, and you may not even have to pay for a calling plan if you use a device that can operate over a Wi-Fi network instead.

As you set up an additional number for your business, also set up rules about which person or people in your organization will be responsible for sending timely responses, and let your clients know that you can offer customer support directly through WhatsApp.

Be sure to include your new number in all of the promotional communication for your business, listing it at the bottom of your emails, on flyers, on your company website, and on your company's profiles for social media sites.

99. Create a strategy for WhatsApp responses from your business

Creating WhatsApp response guidelines can help employees to respond properly and in a timely manner to questions and comments from customers via WhatsApp. WhatsApp responses can be done on a mobile device or through WhatsApp web, found at *https://web.whatsapp.com*, for longer or more detailed responses.

Here are some of the topics your company's WhatsApp guidelines should cover:

- **Who will respond:** Which department or employees are responsible for responding to messages? Do they have access to the materials they will need for accurate responses?

- **How the response is formulated:** It can be helpful to develop some templates for communication, especially for starting and ending conversations. For example, you might create a template to say "Thank you for doing business with us. We're here to serve you in any way we can." Prewritten responses can be stored in a phone or on a computer. Avoid using too many prewritten responses, which can feel unfriendly to a customer.

- **What media will be used:** Photos and videos of your products can be helpful when stored on your phone or computer for easy access. For example, if someone is interested in a rental property from your company, a picture or video can be a better way to share information than writing out a long description. Audio messages can also be an effective tool, when used correctly.

- **What next steps need to be taken:** As a customer becomes interested in a product or service, it's a good idea to have steps in place to encourage them to make a call to continue the transaction.

Most importantly, always make sure to communicate your business hours on WhatsApp, as this will allow consumers to know when they can expect a timely answer from you.

100. Expand your business globally with WhatsApp

JMB Group is an innovative company in Northern Spain offering special cleaning machines for buses and trucks. Earlier, they just used traditional promotion strategies, but a few years back I recommended that they start promoting their WhatsApp number more prominently on their website and on their YouTube videos.

Here is what Claudia Araujo from JMB Group had to say about the benefits WhatsApp has given them:

EXPERT OPINION – Claudia Araujo

"Earlier the only method of contacting us was a phone number, email or a contact form on our website. After we introduced our WhatsApp number and encouraged people to contact us there, all of a sudden we started to receive inquiries all over the world in countries like Brazil, Morocco and Costa Rica. These were people who had seen our products on YouTube or our website, but hadn't contacted us before since making international phone calls is expensive and writing an email is something that takes time when you are on a mobile phone.

To our surprise the use of WhatsApp has given us huge opportunities to expand our business internationally and the additional benefit is that it's so fast so you can immediately respond to people and start building a business relationship. With email communication, that would take a much longer time. At this moment we use WhatsApp in several ways and the following are just some of them:"

- *Send offers to customers who have already bought something from us.*
- *Send links to product videos to interested clients.*
- *When our clients want to order more products they always contact us via WhatsApp.*
- *We also use WhatsApp to communicate with clients to make sure the order has arrived.*

> *"We really appreciate Lasse's recommendation to use WhatsApp and now it helps us to have instant communication with our clients and to work in a more productive way. I encourage all companies to start implementing WhatsApp in their business."*
>
> *Claudia Araujo*
> *JMB Group*
> *www.jmbgrupo.com*

101. Leverage the power of the Facebook ecosystem and take action

I hope you have learned a great number of beneficial tips and strategies on how best to utilize Facebook, Instagram, WhatsApp and Facebook Messenger to benefit your business. One of the key strategies is to design your action plan so that you will use all of these four platforms together in order to achieve the greatest possible impact for your business.

Most of your competitors are probably not taking advantage of the whole Facebook ecosystem – Facebook, Instagram, WhatsApp and Facebook Messenger – simultaneously, but rather maybe just one or two of them at the same time, and it can be extremely beneficial for your business when you leverage the entire ecosystem correctly.

Remember that just reading these tips and strategies is not enough, you actually need to start taking action. I recommend setting apart some time over the next few weeks and planning how you can implement the tips and strategies which are most important for your business.

You might find it useful to use the templates and checklist that I provide as bonuses for the readers of this book. Signup here or visit *www.101fb.com/resources* to download your bonuses.

THREE SUGGESTED ACTION STEPS FROM CHAPTER 10:

Here are three suggested action steps related to the content of this Chapter.

- Make a list of how your company could use Facebook Messenger and what type of content (photos, videos, etc.) could be sent to possible customers. Familiarize yourself with the web interface of Facebook Messenger at *www.messenger.com.*

- Get a separate phone number that can be used for WhatsApp and start to promote it everywhere.

- Start to use WhatsApp, especially with your most loyal customers, and begin to test sending audio messages, as they help you to communicate faster and to generate more trust with users.

HIRE ME TO SPEAK AT YOUR NEXT EVENT

Thank you for considering me as a speaker for your event. I specialize in helping companies and organizations to better understand and implement the latest digital marketing and social media marketing strategies. The audiences usually leave my workshops feeling inspired and entertained, and having learned a lot of very valuable and highly actionable techniques.

I have conducted training and seminars for companies and organizations from many different sectors, and spoken in the United States, England, Spain, Finland, Estonia, Lithuania, Colombia, Honduras, Guatemala, Bolivia, and the Caribbean.

If you want to check my availability for your event, or have any questions, please visit
www.lasserouhiainen.com/speaking

REVIEW THIS BOOK ON AMAZON

If you have found this book to be valuable, please take a brief moment to review it on Amazon. Your feedback will help me to make it even better for future readers.

Thanks and good luck,

Lasse Rouhiainen

You can contact me at *lasse@lasserouhiainen.com*

Made in the USA
Middletown, DE
20 February 2017